# THIRD WORLD WOMEN
## SPEAK OUT

# THIRD WORLD WOMEN
# SPEAK OUT

INTERVIEWS IN SIX COUNTRIES
ON CHANGE, DEVELOPMENT, AND BASIC NEEDS

## Perdita Huston

*With a Foreword by*
## Arvonne S. Fraser

Published in cooperation with the Overseas Development Council
PRAEGER PUBLISHERS
New York • London • Sydney • Toronto

Library of Congress Cataloging in Publication Data

Huston, Perdita
  Third World women speak out.

  1. Underdeveloped areas — Women — Attitudes.
2. Underdeveloped areas — Social conditions.
I. Overseas Development Council. II. Title.
HQ1870.9.H87   301.41'2'091724   78-32180

PRAEGER PUBLISHERS
PRAEGER SPECIAL STUDIES
383 Madison Avenue, New York, N.Y. 10017, U.S.A.

Published in the United States of America in 1979
by Praeger Publishers,
A Division of Holt, Rinehart and Winston, CBS, Inc.

9  038  987654321

For Francoise, Jenny, and Pierre
and the children of the women who speak out
in this book

Cover design by Artwork Unlimited, Inc. Photo credits: cover, World Bank photo by Ivan Massar (Kenya); p. iv, World Bank photo by Tomas Sennett (Sri Lanka); p. xii, World Bank photo by Tomas Sennett (Sri Lanka); p. 2, photo by Hortense Boutell (Egypt); p. 18, World Bank photo by James Pickerell (Kenya); p. 32, photo by Valeriana Kallab (Sri Lanka); p. 46, World Bank photo by Kay Muldoon (Tunisia); p. 64, World Bank photo by Ivan Massar (Kenya); p. 86, International Development Association photo by Kay Muldoon (Tunisia); p. 100, International Labor Office photo (Sri Lanka); p. 114, World Bank photo by Edwin G. Huffman (Mexico); p. 128, United Nations photo (Sudan).

The views expressed in this publication are those of the author and other contributors, and do not necessarily express those of the U.S. Agency for International Development, the Overseas Development Council, or the International Center for Research on Women, or of their directors, officers, or staff.

# Contents

# Acknowledgments

*It would be impossible to name all those who contributed to this volume: the countless individuals who patiently helped me on the field trips abroad and those who, having heard tales of those travels, encouraged me to write about them in this form. To all I owe my gratitude.*

*Individuals who offered special guidance include Arvonne Fraser, Coordinator of the Office of Women in Development of the U.S. Agency for International Development, who provided both financial and intellectual support for this project; Maxine Hitchcock, who, because of her interest in encouraging more published work on the problems and opinions of women in developing countries, urged me to seek the collaboration of the Overseas Development Council in this project; and Mayra Buvinić of the International Center for Research on Women, who sees far beyond words to the real issues. To Page Wilson, Evelyn Harrison, Hortense Boutell, Maryanne Worthing, Diana Michaelis, and Joan Corwin, I am greatly indebted; they gave generously — encouragement and sustenance — throughout the writing of this volume.*

*Tarzie Vittachi, Steve Hellinger, and Denis Goulet, who read the manuscript in its original form, deserve special mention. They urged me to "tell it like it is," regardless of how the text can at times appear unfavorable to the image of men. And to Valeriana Kallab of the Overseas Development Council, I am much obliged. Her advice was invaluable, and her skill and perseverance — and that of her colleagues Nancy Krekeler, Nadine Horenstein, and Mary Westcott — was greatly appreciated.*

PERDITA HUSTON

# THIRD WORLD WOMEN
# SPEAK OUT

# Foreword

*Third World Women Speak Out* is published in the belief that it is important for developers, policymakers, and citizens to hear from the people they are trying to aid. Worldwide, too often, it is the women who are not heard and whose problems are not visible. The U.N. Decade for Women and its World Plan of Action are one expression of the needs and concerns of women. We hope this book, with its different voices, also will be a valuable and instructive document for that growing constituency who are recognizing that women are partners in the development process.

The message of this book is that women in the villages and towns of the developing world are coping with tremendous problems and have a resilience many will admire. They have aspirations for their children, their entire families, and for themselves. They could benefit greatly from assistance on a small scale, pointed at the village and the family, but taking specific account of women and their needs.

Perceptions are changing, but there are still many who suspect that the International Women's Year Conference held in Mexico City in 1975 and its World Plan of Action for the 1976-1985 Decade for Women were the "brainchild" of the women's movement in the developed countries. Many believed that these events and actions inappropriately projected the concerns of Western women on the rest of the world. This charge is easily dispelled by a glance at the actual plan adopted at Mexico City by over one hundred nations — and later ratified in the U.N. General Assembly, which declared 1976-1985 the Decade for Women, with the themes "equality, development, and peace." The Plan is not irrelevant to the problems of women in the developed world, but its focus throughout is *first,* on the problems and needs of people in the world's poor countries, and *second,* on removing the barriers that keep women in these countries from realizing a fair share of the available benefits of development:

> As a result of the uneven development that prevails in international economic relations, three quarters of humanity is faced with urgent and pressing social and economic problems. The women among them are even more affected by such problems, and the new measures taken to improve their situation as well as

their role in the process of development must be an integral part of the global project for the establishment of a new economic order. . . .

While integrated programmes for the benefit of all members of society should be the basis for action in implementing this Plan, special measures on behalf of women whose status is the result of particularly discriminatory attitudes will be necessary.[1]

Clearly there are, as the World Plan of Action acknowledges, major national, and regional, differences in the status of women—differences that are rooted in cultural and political history (including colonialism), in existing political, economic, and social structures, and in widely varying levels of development. These North-South, as well as regional and national differences, are very real and often explode in international forums, as they did initially at the IWY Conference in Mexico City. There are also considerable differences in outlook. Thus while Western women are exploring life options in which motherhood is not always central, such issues do not engage Third World women, whose experience at this stage generally dictates other emphases. At the same time, however, there are basic *similarities* that unite women in striving to eliminate another major set of differences wherever these exist: sex differences in legal, economic, political, and social status. These differences between the rights and opportunities of women and men vary greatly in degree and character from country to country (and even within countries), but they tend to be concentrated in the same areas—in education and training, employment and income, access to services (including health programs), political participation, and legal rights. Thus there are certain commonalities in women's problems regardless of social and economic context — similarities that are very apparent in the expressed concerns of the women who speak out from six different cultural and economic environments in Perdita Huston's book. These similarities, together with a shared commitment to eliminating the causes of the major differences, are at the core of the "women in development" effort, which is an international women's movement and is increasingly emerging as a powerful force for social and economic change in our times.

The major action thrusts of the World Plan drawn up in Mexico City are for: *education and training, employment, health and nutrition, the family in modern society, population, and political action.* The document's broad guidelines are, and should be, useful to development planners in national and international agencies, who must move on to transform the

---

[1]*See World Plan of Action, in* Report of the World Conference of the International Women's Year *(Mexico City, June 19-July 2, 1975), U.N. Publication Sales No. E.76.IV.1 (New York: United Nations, 1976), pp. 9-43. Also reprinted in* Women and World Development, *Irene Tinker and Michèle Bo Bramsen, eds. (Washington, D.C.: Overseas Development Council, 1976), pp. 191-224.*

guidelines into specific targets and policy measures, and implementation and evaluation procedures. It is interesting that the women who speak out in this book convey most of the same messages on priority needs as the World Plan of Action—but they do so far more directly and poignantly, by helping us to see the problems, and to envision their possible solutions, in the human context of these women's everyday lives.

The women say that what they need is education and training—to earn cash to enable their families to subsist, yes, but also to emerge out of the "prison" of their ignorance, to assume more meaningful and effective roles in their families and societies. These concerns echo the World Plan's recognition that in many countries, girls and women are at a marked disadvantage in education. As the Plan states—and as the tables in Annex B of this volume also indicate for the six countries in which Huston interviewed women — "illiteracy is much more widespread among women than among men, and the rates are generally higher in rural than in urban areas." Women's illiteracy and lack of training in basic skills contribute especially acutely—through no fault of their own — to the "vicious circle of underdevelopment, low productivity, and poor conditions of health and welfare" in a great many countries.

It is often asserted that education creates the motivation for change. Interestingly, the interviews in this book suggest that the motivation for change often is there already, even at very low education levels — suggesting the vast unchanneled potential for development—but that education and training are desperately needed to make that motivation effective.

The great and surprisingly articulate concern of the women in this book about their economic roles also supports the World Plan's strong argument for recognition and enhancement of women's productive roles. The Plan urges governments and development agencies to take measures to ease the drudgery and increase the efficiency of women's work, to ameliorate the unreasonably heavy "double" work load (compared to that of men) that falls upon large groups of women in many countries, and to help women to acquire and strengthen their *income*-generating skills. In many countries, women's traditional economic roles confine them to tasks which, however critical to society—for example, the production, processing, storage, and preparation of food at the family level—are not remunerated in cash and reinforce their low status in increasingly monetized economies. This is an especially grave problem where the migration of men to cities in search of cash income is a massive, socially disruptive pattern that is leaving more and more rural women the actual heads of households, but without a source of income adequate to assure even the minimum basic needs of their young and old dependents.

The World Plan points to the special disadvantages that rural women workers experience — in access to technology, education and training, credit, and marketing skills—in carrying out their traditionally important role in agricultural production and in the processing and marketing of food. The Plan also notes and calls for reforms of the situation of women workers in industry, arguing that at present women workers suffer especially severely from the impact of unemployment, inflation, the lack of public funds for education and medical care in their societies, and the uncontrolled proliferation of the problems of migration and the total urban environment.

What the women in this volume say about education and work appears to be in agreement with the education policy emphasis articulated in 1977 by World Bank President Robert McNamara and now supported in principle—but still far from adequately implemented—by many development planners:

> A basic learning package, for both men and women, including functional literacy and numeracy, some choice of relevant vocational skills for productive activity, family planning and health, child care, nutrition, sanitation, and the knowledge required for active civic participation is an investment no nation can afford not to make. The very nature of the educational process imposes a relatively long time lag for the economic return on that investment. But if the basic package is right, the return will be huge. And not the least component of that return will be the benefit of reduced fertility.[2]

The trust that many of the women place in the ability of women's organizations to help them is also instructive. Women's groups of various kinds, formal and informal, exist in almost every community and within every level of society in the developing world (as well as in the industrialized world). In the developing countries, many of these women's groups are already conducting small projects on a village or regional level, but they need assistance — small grants and technical assistance. Little attention has been paid to these groups as vehicles for development. Donor-country development planners — as well as feminists in the Western countries — tend to discount them, arguing that they are largely ineffective (politically and economically) and tend to reinforce the existing separatism of the sexes as well as of social classes. But organizational leadership and participatory skills are learned and taught through *groups*. These skills are as important for women as they are for men, and they are a necessity for national development. Unless a populace has trained and experienced leadership, development flounders. Working in groups brings women a sense of control over their own destinies and provides support for a common purpose. Women's organizations can thus serve a dual purpose of teaching skills to *individuals*

---

[2]*Robert S. McNamara*, Accelerating Population Stabilization Through Social and Economic Progress, *Development Paper 24 (Washington, D.C.: Overseas Development Council, 1977), p. 29.*

while enhancing perspectives on the economic and social prospects for the whole *group*. They can, and in many countries do, serve an important *transitional* role — and possibly even as an effective long-term force.

Links need to be forged among women's groups within developing countries, among developing countries within the various geographic regions, and among developing and developed countries — for both technical assistance and political reasons. Some of these links are already established, but generally on a small scale, and the women's organizations are usually operating on very limited budgets.

Over the next eighteen months, development planners and political representatives alike—meeting in national, regional, and international agencies and forums, and finally in the 1980 special session of the U.N. General Assembly on development cooperation—will engage in what promises to be an intensive attempt to set targets and mobilize action for social and economic development in the 1980s and beyond. This exercise —which will look ahead to the year 2000 and try to improve on the now rather dated blueprint for the Second U.N. Development Decade of the 1970s—overlaps with the U.N. Decade for Women 1976-1985. A World Conference of the U.N. Decade for Women, with a special focus on employment, health, and education, is scheduled for 1980 in Copenhagen; its task will be to examine the progress made in the implementation of the Plan since 1975 and to adapt and focus strategies for the years ahead.

The concurrent scheduling of these two exercises in international planning and commitment — one to shape the general, international strategy for the Third U.N. Development Decade, the other to help eliminate the specific development problems confronting *women* — presents planners with a very great opportunity. A *serious* attempt to integrate these two parallel paths of targeted planning for the 1980s—and to do so in very specific terms—could do much to assure both economic growth and social justice. It could improve the quality of life of women, men, and children in all countries.

The economic and social problems and partial solutions that are expressed so directly by the Third World women who speak out in this volume are not "women's issues" alone, but rather an important challenge to be met in the design and implementation of any *effective* strategy of development.

The project leading to the publication of this book began with Perdita Huston's own sense of mission to find ways for the people at the grass roots of development—both *women* and men—to express directly their own ideas about the problems they confront and possible solutions. A free-lance American journalist until her recent appointment to a Peace Corps regional directorship, Huston had already completed one manuscript on her interviews with women in the same six developing countries when she came to see us at A.I.D. That manuscript, prepared for the U.N. Fund for Population Activities, focused on women's views on family planning. It later appeared as *Message from the Village* (The Epoch B Foundation, 1978). Huston's proposal to the Office of Women in Development at A.I.D. was to use the voluminous additional material she had gathered in the course of her interviews to write another, more wide-ranging book on the views of these women on change, development, and basic needs. She believed that such a book could be of value to those who plan policy for many other economic and social sectors besides family planning — and that it would interest a much broader audience.

Huston's proposal led to a collaborative venture involving the A.I.D. Office of Women in Development, the International Center for Research on Women (ICRW), and the Overseas Development Council (ODC). Huston herself wanted the tapes of her interviews to be systematically analyzed by social scientists to provide an independent assessment to complement her own experiential, journalistic presentation. The results of this analysis, conducted by Mayra Buvinić and other researchers at the ICRW and funded by the Office of Women in Development, are published as Annex A to this volume.

Huston came to the Women in Development Office knowing that one of its main concerns is to prepare and publish materials that illustrate women's roles and status in the developing world. Developers need to know what women do in various cultures and regions, what their aspirations and hopes are, and what they think could be done to improve their individual lot and to help their country. Some of the recent publications of the Office include: *Women and Food* (proceedings and papers of the Tucson Conference); *Images of Women in the Literature of Selected Developing Countries — Ghana, Senegal, Haiti, Jamaica; Women-Headed Households — The Ignored Factor in Development Planning;* the *International Directory of Women's Development Organizations;* and a condensed version of the World Plan of Action in English, French, and Spanish.

The Overseas Development Council seemed a natural partner for the project, in view of its two earlier, widely disseminated books on women and development issues: *Women and World Development* (1976), which it published in collaboration with the Office of International Science of the American Association for the Advancement of Science, and *Development As If Women Mattered: An Annotated Bibliography with a Third World Focus* (1978), published in cooperation with the Secretariat for Women in Development of the New TransCentury Foundation. The ODC's President, James P. Grant, and Valeriana Kallab, its Executive Editor, brought to the project their enthusiasm and commitment to publishing Huston's proposed book to round out ODC's continuing contribution to inquiry about, and improvement of, the status of women. Collaboration with ODC also subsequently led to the involvement of Praeger Publishers, through the interest of Ellen Lazer, acquiring Editor for Praeger's growing list of publications on women's issues.

Perdita Huston and I wish to gratefully acknowledge the contributions of all who had a part in the project. With some amusement, I also must mention that this volume is yet another product of women's work —in authorship, support, editing, and publication. But as is true of most women's labor, it is for us all: men, women, and children. Our hope is that *people* will benefit—that women and men will become equal partners in the work of development.

ARVONNE S. FRASER
*Coordinator, Office of Women in Development*
*U.S. Agency for International Development*

January 1979

# 1

## PREFACE

# "Now go back and tell"

PREFACE

This book has one objective: to arouse more public and professional sensitivity to the realities of women's lives in the developing nations. It is an attempt to express my concern about the impact of the development process on the family unit and on its individual members.

Development is a process that brings with it enormous changes in the very substance of people's lives. It touches their values, their cultural norms, and their perceptions of one another. It can bring an opportunity for personal growth and social harmony, or, tragically, it can tear the social fabric asunder.

Years ago, as a medical-social worker in North Africa, I had an opportunity to observe the influence of development programs on rural family life. I was particularly impressed by the effects of those programs on the lives of women and children. It seemed to me that the more negative implications of the programs were not perceived at the planning level. Since that time, I have wanted to provide a vehicle by which women might speak for themselves about the pressures they face in rapidly changing environments. Their views would surely help to identify the problems at hand and thereby assist in the improvement of policy design.

## A Six-Country Mission

The opportunity to record the conversations on which I draw in this book was made possible by a grant from the U.N. Fund for Population Activities (UNFPA). The countries I visited — Tunisia, Egypt, Sudan, Kenya, Sri Lanka, and Mexico — were selected by UNFPA for their cultural, social, political, and environmental as well as economic diversity. It should be noted, however, that five of these countries rank among the world's very poor nations, with their per capita GNP ranging from Sri Lanka's $200 per year to Tunisia's $840 per year; only Mexico, with its annual per capita GNP of $1,090, ranks among the relatively better-off developing countries.*

---

*Annex B of this volume (pp. 149-152) presents some social and economic indicators of variations in the quality of life among the selected six countries.

My mission was to travel to these nations and discuss with women their views on family size and the desirability of family planning services. The results of my inquiry have been published in a book issued by the UNFPA.* But to gather views on such a sensitive subject, I first had to understand the factors that contribute to those views: the elements of a woman's life that contribute to her perception of the needs of her family and to her personal aspirations. That wider-ranging inquiry into women's perceptions and aspirations is the subject of this volume.

Upon arrival in each nation, I met first with government and U.N. officials, who briefed me on the development policies and projects of the country. A second series of meetings, arranged through women friends of different nations, led me to women leaders known for their work both *with* and *for* women and for their independent thinking. Although these women in many instances belong to the upper classes in their societies (as do most university-educated women and men in developing countries), and might therefore be suspected of having little knowledge of the situation of the poorer classes, I found that their perceptions almost always were grounded in the stark realities facing poor families. Many were initiators of progressive efforts for the advancement of women, and their words contribute significantly to this book.

Based on the recommendations of both groups — officials and women leaders — I organized trips to rural areas and small urban centers. Traveling by bus, train, car, and mostly by landrover, I made a consistent attempt to visit areas judged to be "not worth the time" by officials; I systematically avoided the "showcase" locales. On several occasions, I encountered frowns and mockery on the part of officials; they seemed perplexed by my request — my insistence — to talk with those they judged "only poor and ignorant women." The experience taught me that the tendency to discount the opinions of the poor (and women) is found at local as well as national and international levels.

The first country I visited was Tunisia. Once a key contributor to ancient Rome's granary, Tunisia still is predominantly an agricultural nation. Today its principal products are wheat, olives, and citrus fruits. Most of the country is favored with a mild Mediterranean climate. Only its southern portion, bordering on the Sahara Desert, is infertile. There, the population lives in oases or continues centuries-old nomadic wanderings with the changing seasons.

When I had lived and worked in Tunisia sixteen years prior to this assignment, the country's population had numbered four million people. By mid-1976, the count was nearing six million. Tunisia's "population pyramid" confirms that it is a youthful nation: 43.2 per cent of Tunisians are under age fifteen.

When I arrived in Tunisia, the National Population Council graciously provided me with a car and driver to enable me to travel to the more remote parts of the country to talk with women. During the first

---

*Perdita Huston, Message from the Village *(New York: The Epoch B Foundation, 1978).*

five days, I traveled south along the coast to the ancient fortified city of Sfax, and from there to villages hidden among the vast olive groves that cover the Sahel region. The following week was spent in the northwestern region, visiting villages nestled among rolling wheat fields near the hillside city of Le Kef. The route to Le Kef was lined not only with towering columns of ancient Roman towns, whose ruins are scattered throughout the small nation, but also with the tents of nomads who had fled the dry season in the south.

Members of the National Union of Tunisian Women — an active women's organization of over 40,000 members — welcomed me in each region, and their briefings were most useful. Wherever I traveled in Tunisia, officials were helpful and concerned about the success of my mission. Once again I experienced the legendary hospitality of Tunisia's people. In Sfax, for example, Georgette Cheour (a midwife) and her husband, Mohamed (a paramedic), insisted that I take all meals in their home. I learned much from them about the issues facing the poorer families of the region.

Among Moslem nations, Tunisia sets a bright example in providing the legal basis for the integration of women into national life. Under the leadership of President Habib Bourguiba, the Tunisian National Assembly passed the Personal Status Code shortly after Tunisia gained independence from France in 1956. This code prohibits polygamy, defines court procedures for divorce, grants universal suffrage, and requires the consent of both parties to a marriage. With this one law, women became equal to men before the courts.

Everywhere I traveled in Tunisia, women spoke gratefully of Bourguiba's leadership in "giving us our rights." The president of the National Union of Tunisian Women, Fathia M'Zali, stated that "President Bourguiba is the only *unconditional* feminist I have known." She explained that the President has made a practice of speaking out against traditions that hinder the full participation of women in Tunisian society. His personal commitment to resolving this problem, she maintained, has resulted in a significant change in people's attitudes. On the streets of Tunisia's cities, women no longer veil their faces. Youthful men and women walk together in the streets, a sight unknown twenty years ago. Female police officers direct traffic in downtown Tunis — a visible symbol of Tunisia's efforts to involve women in many aspects of public life.

Despite the considerable changes that have taken place in Tunisia — as in the other countries visited — I was to hear tales of disregard for laws defining the rights of women. Several teenage girls told me that they knew they would not be allowed to choose their husbands, even though the law stipulates that both bride and bridegroom must consent to the marriage. Traditional practices still prevail in many other fields as well. In primary school, for example, girls represent only 39 per cent of students, and at the university level, even less — only 25 per cent. These statistics show a great increase from those of twenty years ago, but, as many women pointed out, "We still have a long way to go." What remains unique about modern Tunisia is that for the past twenty years, the nation's leaders have actively supported women's participation in Tunisian society.

A flight across Libya took me to Egypt, the most populous of Arab nations, and to the Nile-side city of Cairo. Of forty million Egyptians, 99 per cent inhabit only 3.5 per cent of the country's total surface; they live along the Nile River and its delta, where crops of cotton, wheat, and rice can be grown. The remainder of the country is largely desert, dotted with widely scattered oases.

Although influential communities of Christians and Jews have existed in Egypt for centuries, the great majority of Egyptians are Moslems. Islam has greatly affected customs and laws, and Moslem religious leaders are very influential. I was told by many women that the barriers to women's advancement tended to be sustained not so much by law as by religious leaders. Since 1919, when they first joined in street demonstrations to protest oppressive British Protectorate policy, Egyptian women have been involved in a struggle for their rights. The highly educated urban population, concentrated mainly in Cairo and Alexandria, has a large contingent of politically conscious and active women. Equal pay, voting rights, and civil liberties are ensured by law, although I was told by many women that customs and traditions still inhibit women's participation in activities outside the home. One woman official, noting that 50 per cent of Egyptian women remain illiterate, commented: "Our women do not even know they have certain rights. We, the educated women, must teach them. This is our job." Jehan Sadat, wife of Egypt's president and herself a social activist, spoke of the uphill battle of promoting women's rights, commenting that "the men don't pay as much attention as they should to the issue."

The Cairo Women's Organization arranged my visit to a village sixty miles northwest of Cairo, where life at first appeared quite traditional, but where the impact of change upon the lives of the younger generation also was visible. Many teenage girls were attending school, although they were still wearing full-length black veils. Some young women even traveled miles from the village each day to attend training courses.

Next I journeyed further north by train for a three-day visit to the Mediterranean port of Alexandria. There, the privately managed Family Planning Association organized visits to health clinics, day-care centers, and youth training courses, at each of which I met women who talked willingly about their family situations and their views.

The following week, I traveled past the Giza pyramids to Fayoum, a region consisting of over 160 village oases spread along a vast irrigation system in the desert southwest of Cairo. As we passed the irrigated fields, we saw a group of children, seven or eight years old, working among the rows of plants under the supervision of an older man. It was there, in Fayoum, that I heard family planning workers make a plea for mechanized farming, saying, "If the farmers had less need of labor in the field, they would have fewer children."

It was not until I flew south from Cairo to Khartoum and viewed the inhospitable vastness of Sudan, that I began to comprehend the magnitude of the problems facing its people. Sudan is the largest nation in

Africa; deserts of sand and rock, bare mountains, vast swamps, and savanna cover 967,500 square miles—an area almost one third the size of the continental United States. Eighty per cent of Sudan's eighteen million people live in isolated rural areas, where the lack of roads and communications is a major barrier to adequate health and educational services.

The country's capital, Khartoum, which calls to mind romantic images of the joining of the Blue and White Niles, is in reality a stark and dusty town to which the poor migrate when they flee even drier regions. Doctors with whom I spoke estimated that 87 per cent of Sudanese children are undernourished and that 80 per cent of the women are anemic. The "population pyramid" is even younger than that of Tunisia, with 45 per cent of Sudan's people under age fourteen. Primary school enrollment stands at only 38 per cent of school-age children, and twice as many boys as girls are enrolled. Illiteracy among Sudanese women is estimated at 95 per cent.

It is often said that there are, in fact, many Sudans. The isolation of towns and the division of the country by the great Sudd swamp contribute to the diversity among tribes and their customs. The north is largely Arab-African and of the Moslem faith. The south, which has its own territorial parliament, is inhabited mostly by Nilotic Africans who either are animists or belong to a variety of Christian sects.

From Khartoum, I traveled by plane northeast to Port Sudan, which lies on the Red Sea and is Sudan's link to the world. Our plane followed the tracks of the railway that is the country's lifeline, spanning the desert that separates Port Sudan from Khartoum. In most areas of northern Sudan, the key to daily survival is water. One woman whom I visited in her hut south of Port Sudan told me she walked three miles each day to fetch water, which then had to be carefully distilled to lessen its salt content. From the rusty tin can that served as the family's cup, I drank of the water that represented hours of patient work.

Later, again from Khartoum, I flew south to Juba. Although it is the largest town in southern Sudan, Juba is but an overgrown village, accessible from the capital only by air or by a month-long boat trip up the White Nile. In the southern region, where the climate is tropical, water is plentiful but carries diseases common to other tropical regions. Bilharzia, malaria, and tuberculosis abound among the region's tribes. A doctor in Juba confirmed that most women in the south are seriously anemic.

From Khartoum itself, I made several trips—to villages in the city's outer reaches and later also to Gezira Province further to the south. I visited villages hidden away along the route to El Medani, a small city that is the heart of the Gezira Scheme, a vast irrigation project. In one village I witnessed the opening of a primary school. While the officials spoke, women sat listening on one side, men on the other. One speaker was a young woman whose veil—which in Sudan covers the head and body but rarely the face—was made of white cotton imprinted with the International Women's Year symbol. Later she told me that the women's group in El Medani had designed the material and produced hundreds of such veils during 1975. I found, however, that in northern Sudan women were far more reticent in expressing their perceptions of their status and roles than women in the other countries I visited. In the southern region of the country, the contrary was true; there I found that women were aware of and outspoken about women's potential contribution to their community and nation.

In Khartoum, several educated women refused to let me tape our conversation; others requested that a witness be present during the discussions. I sensed, however, that the major reason for this was a feeling of insecurity about discussing the situation of women with a foreign visitor rather than personal timidity.

As I flew south from Juba to Nairobi, Kenya's plateau-perched capital—which I had visited several years before—I was once again brought back to the realities of the country's geography. There is very little of the lush vegetation that the wildlife films shown in the West mislead us to associate with Kenya. In fact, 80 per cent of the country's surface is marginal land, and the past few years had not brought much rainfall even to the more fertile areas. During this visit, I saw evidence everywhere of prolonged drought. The scope of this disaster becomes clearer when one realizes that most of Kenya's thirteen million people subsist on what they grow for consumption. Even the animals were suffering. One day during the drive to Mombasa, I spotted groups of elephants plodding along in search of food. Their rib cages were poking through the heavy skin that hung loosely from their emaciated bodies.

Compared to Sudan, however, Kenya appears quite well off. It has been the scene of rapid foreign investment, and the country's capital exhibits all the external markings of a modern city. If one looks more closely, however, one finds that Nairobi is burdened with the afflictions of other large urban centers. As many as 300,000 people — nearly one third of Nairobi's total population — live in slums of cardboard and tin shanties. Poverty, prostitution, and fear are now a part of the capital's offerings to those who continue to migrate to its outskirts.

The changes brought about by the rapidly growing economy have profoundly affected the nation's social structures. One third of all rural households are headed by women, largely because men have migrated to the cities and towns in the hope of finding salaried work. Their wives continue to work the family plots of land and are always busy with some scheme to earn a bit of cash. Everywhere one sees women walking to market with basketloads of vegetables on their heads, infants strapped to their backs, and older children following behind. Even while they walk to market, these women often are weaving baskets or fashioning other handiwork that they hope to exchange for cash needed for the family's support or the children's education. In Kenya, schooling is free only until the fifth grade, and throughout my travels, I heard women express anxiety about their need to find ways to earn cash to equip and send their children to school.

The women of Kenya — whether Christian, animist, or Moslem — enjoy far more mobility than their Moslem sisters to the north. As several women leaders pointed out, however, "We still have little legal freedom.

We are dominated by males through a lack of legislation that would protect us from unjust divorce, polygamy, or unfair inheritance practices and abandonment."

Throughout Kenya, I found agency officials very helpful; family planning associations, offices of U.N. agencies, women's organizations, and government ministries provided me with a car and driver and aided my travels to the provinces. Over a three-week period, I visited the regions between Mombasa on the Indian Ocean and Busia on the Ugandan border. In each village, town, farm, school, and plantation on my itinerary, I was guided by community development workers, social workers, paramedics, or members of *Maendeleo ya Wanawake*, the major national women's organization.

From Nairobi I flew to Colombo, Sri Lanka (long known to the rest of the world as Ceylon). Centuries of Arab, Portuguese, and British domination have left their marks on Sri Lankan life and culture. Buddhism is the predominant religion, but Hinduism, Islam, and Christianity also have greatly influenced the national culture. With a population of fourteen million — some 514 persons per square mile — Sri Lanka is one of the world's most densely populated nations.

The most noticeable differences between Sri Lanka and the other nations I visited seem mainly to result from the country's remarkable educational, medical, and transportation systems. Education for boys and girls — from primary school through university levels — has been free for the past thirty years. The literacy rates are 89 per cent for men and 72 per cent for women. Compared to those of other developing countries, the medical infrastructure of Sri Lanka is exceptional; there is one doctor for every five thousand inhabitants, and 55 per cent of all births take place in medical facilities. Public transportation is remarkably efficient; the island is crisscrossed with hundreds of roadways on which some eleven thousand buses carry over a million people each day. The railway system stretches across the entire island and climbs into the tea-covered highlands (through some of the most beautiful terrain on earth). Despite this remarkable infrastructure, Sri Lankans nonetheless face — although perhaps to a lesser degree — many of the problems common to other developing nations. Unemployment, for example, stands at a chronic 14 per cent of the total work force; and in 1974, 14 per cent of all preschool children suffered from third-degree protein-calorie malnutrion.

I traveled by train to several small towns north of Colombo to visit a series of cooperative farms; one was managed by young people, another by older workers who had been employed on the estate before it had been nationalized and turned into a cooperative settlement. Accompanied by members of the *Mahila Samithi* (a women's organization), I also visited villages in the Colombo area in which women's employment projects were being supported and directed by the organization's membership. Several days later, officials of the Office of Family Planning took me by car to the plantation country high in the central region of the

9

island. We traveled out from the ancient capital of Kandy and from the town of Maskeliya to the region's plantations and villages. On one plantation, when visiting a class in an open-structure school building equipped only with hand-hewn benches, I asked the schoolmaster who among the students sitting before me was the brightest pupil and the best worker. "*She* is," he answered without hesitation, pointing to an eleven-year-old girl. The child blushed and partly hid her face in her arms while smiling—an expression of the modesty found among Sri Lankans of all ages.

My Sri Lankan travels extended as far as Kankesanturai on the northernmost tip of the island, where I traveled by train, crossing "the dry zone" — a vast area that had not benefited from a monsoon for several years. From the train I could see hundreds of abandoned huts—left by those who had fled the drought for more fertile regions.

Although the women of Sri Lanka have far better access to education than women in the other countries I visited — female literacy is 72 per cent—taboos and superstitions continue to restrict the lives of many, especially in rural areas. Everywhere, the dowry plays an important role in women's lives as well. In Sri Lanka, it is generally the bride's family that provides the dowry to attract a husband; the less educated the girl, the more dowry she must offer to compensate, it is said, "for her ignorance."

While it is true that many of the women I talked with in my travels, in the rural areas especially, evidenced poor self-esteem, I found Sri Lankan women to be more politically aware than women in, for example, Tunisia, Sudan, or Mexico. Many are involved in trade-union and other political activity, as well as in women's organizations, which play an important role by serving the rural poor.

The last country I visited was Mexico. Although Mexico's per capita GNP statistics suggest that it is a relatively richer country, the disparities between the quality of life of the upper and lower classes are far more evident there than in the other countries I visited. I did not find social consciousness as widespread among upper-class women as, for example, in Sri Lanka. It did not prove easy to locate women who worked with less fortunate women — perhaps partly because I visited Mexico at a time when the new government was in its first months and information on who would be working in what field was not readily available.

The National Population Council and a handful of concerned women in Mexico City helped me plan trips to rural areas near the cities of Oaxaca and Guanajuato, to the suburbs of Mexico City, and to the vast lake-bed squatter settlement of Netzahualcoyotl. There, two million people — recent migrants from rural areas — huddle together without the barest amenities.

Rapid population growth—the population of Mexico is now sixty-two million and is expected to double before the end of the century — has resulted in the migration of millions of peasants to urban areas. In the capital alone, one thousand migrants arrive each day. In 1900, 81 per cent of all Mexicans lived in rural areas; today the figure has decreased to 41 per cent. Women account for some 55 per cent of the migrants from rural to urban areas. They leave the villages seeking employment, often as domestic servants. When they do not find such work in the cities, they face few alternatives. If they are young, they frequently turn to prostitution; if not, they often resort to begging in the streets. Homeless peasant women, often carrying small children, roam every quarter of Mexico City. Official statistics say that unmarried women account for 28 per cent of all births in Mexico; it is also estimated that over one million clandestine abortions are performed each year.

As I traveled throughout Mexico, women often named the church and the all-powerful "macho" mentality as the reasons for their lack of autonomy and for their reluctance to act independently on any matter, including family planning.

Proximity to the United States is an ever-present factor of Mexican life. In Dolores Hidalgo, I met a peasant woman who admired her husband greatly because he had illegally crossed the U.S. border, located hundreds of miles to the north, seventeen times in search of work. The longest he ever had been able to work before being apprehended was two months. "But," she said, "it meant a lot of money for us." On the other side of Guanajuato, in Villagran, the men migrate because only seasonal work is to be found locally. Miles of strawberry fields surround the village; the delicate fruit is shipped by refrigerated truck to supermarkets in the United States. Yet in Villagran, both children and adults suffer from severe nutritional deficiencies as export crops take the place of local staple crops.

### The Search for a Genuine Exchange

Even this very sketchy account of my interviewing itinerary gives some sense of the enormous diversity of the countries I visited. The nearly two hundred women I spoke with in the six countries were hardly a homogeneous group. In addition to the diversity of cultures in which they were rooted, they differed from one another in numerous other ways—they were both rural and urban women, they were both illiterate and educated, and they were both poor and rich.

Nevertheless, if I focused on their differences, I would be going directly counter to the cumulative character and impact of what they said, which is what I wish to share with the readers of this book. What is surprising is that when women in these very different places spoke of the issues that concerned them, the similarities in what they observed seemed to outweigh differences. Rural women, especially, emphasized similar needs: they spoke of the problems they continue to face in the form of social practices that limit their personal roles and influence in the family and community; of their heavy work burden and extreme fatigue; of their inability to earn enough, if any, cash; and of their desire to learn and work and educate their children for "a better life than mine."

In my selections of vignettes from the conversations, I do not attempt to provide a scientific sampling of the opinions of women in the six countries.* Rather, I wish to convey what even precise transcripts of interviews cannot communicate: the urgency that the women themselves attributed — by gesture, tone, and repetition itself — to the points they themselves chose to emphasize. In that sense, my method is akin to that of a documentary filmmaker. I am sharing what I personally found persuasive.

Preferring the conversational mode to the structured interview technique, I used no formal questionnaire. We were simply women talking together. In a cattle field in Kenya, beside a tea bush in Sri Lanka, or sheltered from the sun in a palm-roofed hut in Sudan, we discussed our families and our lives. I told about my mother; they told about theirs. They questioned me about my children and spoke with pride about their own.

The majority of the conversations were taped. In a few cases, women refused to be recorded, fearing their husbands' disapproval or the political implications of the words they spoke; they did not, however, object to the use of what they said in this book. In other cases, taping was impossible due to the noise surrounding us — children playing, street sounds, or curious crowds waiting outside to take a look at the "visitor"; but the content of those interviews contributes to this volume as well.

The greatest challenge lay in finding, or creating, an environment in which women would speak with as little reservation as possible. Believing that a group setting would provide a more open and secure atmosphere for conversation, I sought to find women in groups—gathering at a health center, selling in a market, or simply working in the fields. If we talked in a group first—discussing the object of my visit, exchanging stories, and getting to know one another — the women soon became confident and participated readily in the exchange. Following the collective discussions, I asked if anyone wished to pursue the conversation in private. This question always drew more offers than could be pursued because of the time constraints of the women's work responsibilities as well as my own schedule. Thus self-selection played a very important part in determining who would be interviewed. Some readers may consider this a shortcoming of the representativeness of the interviews whose content I share in this volume; this is not my own view. I believe that the self-selection process permitted more open conversations — more "heart-to-heart" talks — than if I had imposed a dialogue on an unwilling person. Moreover, asking for volunteers made it possible for me to ensure some diversity of interviewees; for example, when eight out of twenty women present volunteered to speak with me in private, I was able to choose three of varying ages, or four or five of varying levels of education or training.

The key question I asked was, at least at face value, a simple one: "How does your life differ from that of your mother or grandmother?" The responses triggered discussion on a variety of issues: housing, food,

---

*At the same time, I wished to provide a check on this method —for myself as well as others —and therefore turned over all my interview transcripts to the International Center for Research on Women in Washington, D.C., for analysis according to generally accepted behavioral science techniques. A summary of this analysis is provided in Annex A (pp. 127-149) of this volume.

alcoholism, politics, male-female relationships, children, education, love, and disappointment. In the course of comparing past and present conditions, women began to articulate the needs and the difficulties they encounter in a changing environment.

Because the average discussion took well over an hour, the presentation here of entire conversations is not possible. In excerpting from them, I have tried to communicate as closely as possible the spirit of the entire discussion. It must, of course, be recognized that the personalities and skills of interpreters inevitably influence many aspects of the information gathered. I believe that I was fortunate to find female interpreters who warmed to the subject of my inquiry and who took special care to set the women interviewed at ease. Yet each interpreter differed from the next. Their educational levels varied greatly; they were social workers, members of women's organizations, doctors, teachers, and university students. In some cases, two interpreters were required: one who understood the tribal tongue and could translate it into the national language and another who could translate from the national language into French or English, which I could understand. These translations were sometimes unavoidably awkward. In some cases, moreover, the more abstract expressions of educated interviewers undoubtedly altered the flavor of language used by articulate but uneducated rural women; such losses are unfortunate, but they can at best be minimized. In the belief that on the whole, authenticity would suffer most if the language were heavily altered, the conversations have been edited for comprehension purposes only.

Because what the women interviewed said often was very personal in substance, the question of anonymity was extremely important. I found that most women were willing to speak more freely if they were confident that their words would not be repeated to their family or friends. For this reason, I chose interpreters who were not from the same locality. In a further attempt to assure interviewees of their anonymity, I did not *ask* the women to provide their names. Those who *wished* to tell me their names when I told them mine of course did so, but not in response to any direct request. The reader will find, then, that some women are named in the text while others are not. The more educated women are named because they spoke as leaders, "for the record." They pointed out the need for an exchange of information among women of different nations and hoped to make a contribution to that exchange through their words.

The format of this book is shaped by the common topical threads that emerged during our discussions. The first three chapters reveal the impact of change on women's lives, the effect these changes are having on traditional family relationships, and the social practices that seem to block women's advancement. The content of these three chapters often is startling, dismal, even hopeless. In a sense, it conveys the "psychological" setting I encountered in many of my conversations. The content of the next three chapters — which focus on what the women said about health, nutrition, and family planning; about education and work; and about participation in the community and society at large — often provides a strikingly positive contrast to the first three chapters. While the greatest common concern of the women interviewed was for the future of the family as its members are bombarded with a myriad factors of rapid change during the "development" process, the outlook of most of the women was remarkably positive — despite the enormous barriers that many of them recognized as standing in the way of their aspirations.

In reading the interviews, the reader will, I hope, be compelled to ask the question: Had men also been interviewed, would their views conflict with or give credence to those expressed by the women? In my opinion, this question is a very important one. If similar work on the situation of women is undertaken in the future, care should be given to gathering the views of men as well as women. This could best be done, I believe, by teams of female and male interviewers, for in most rural areas of the developing world today, women interviewers cannot expect to discuss personal and intimate questions openly with men.

The warmth, sincerity, and openness of the women I interviewed were often overwhelming. Nearly all of them expressed curiosity and concern about women in other parts of the world. They wanted to know more about the lives of women because, they said, they cared about them. This "caring" was particularly evident in an experience I had in central Kenya.

A cold winter drizzle was falling on Nyeri when I arrived late one morning. A meeting with a group of fifty older women had been arranged in the unheated town hall. The women were poor and illiterate, but anxious to learn new skills by attending a town-sponsored education group to which I had been invited. I told them (as I did each group with which I met) that I had come to collect their words — that the United Nations had sent me there to listen to them so that they could help me write a book. The book, I explained, would be about women's lives and about the changes, needs, and aspirations of those lives. I would take their words back home, where they would be published so that women and men around the world would better understand the lives and needs of women like themselves.

After an hour of group discussion, I asked if anyone would like to talk with me further, to tell her own story in private. I chose four women from among the volunteers, thanked the group for their participation, and spent the next three hours interviewing in a small office-like room adjoining the hall.

When, much later, I emerged from the building with the last interviewee, all the women with whom I had met hours before were still there, standing in the rain, without shoes or coats, shivering in the winter cold. They had waited for me to complete my work in order to wish me farewell and a good journey. I was distressed and embarrassed: I had had no idea they were waiting for me. I thought they had gone home once the group discussions ended. It seemed they had warmed to my mission. As I moved toward the group, they began to sing and dance. The interpreter explained that they wanted to make me an honorary member of their tribe and to give me a tribal name.

In the midst of the ceremony, a seventy-year-old woman — toothless, shoeless, and in rags—rushed out of the crowd and took me by the arm. Grinning and shaking her finger in my face, she said, with authority: "Now you go back and tell the women in your place that the women of Nyeri *care* about them."

# 2

POSITIVE AND NEGATIVE PERCEPTIONS OF CHANGE

# "Life is more difficult than before"

## POSITIVE AND NEGATIVE PERCEPTIONS OF CHANGE

Just a generation or two ago, the individual's universe in most of the rural areas of the developing countries I visited was limited to the immediate surroundings. Duties and responsibilities were defined by customs and traditions that had evolved over many generations. Men and women had defined roles and status that gave them authority within the family and society; old and young knew their rights and responsibilities. The family was the central unit of social organization, and the economy of the village or region was built upon family subsistence farming. Either husband or wife, or both, worked in the fields. Rural life was based on the barter system. In exchange for precious salt, one offered dried meat or grain, and for medicinal herbs, perhaps food or a jug of the local brew. In exchange for a bride, one gave her parents cattle, sheep, or goats. Where it was customary for the bride's family to provide the dowry, a house was built for the couple, or the bridegroom was given land.

The cash crop system, established extensively under colonialism, and the haphazard evolution from a subsistence economy to a cash economy, have introduced some dramatic dislocations in social structures, attitudes, and values. Among these effects are changes in the traditional division of labor between the sexes. Work for cash generally has been made more accessible to men because — unlike the women, whose traditional tasks have kept them close to the household — they have been more free to move about. As men have taken up work for pay and abandoned their tasks as farmers or shepherds, their work, of necessity, has been assumed by other family members. Often the brunt of the additional chores has been taken up by women. To their traditional tasks, women in many areas have added, for example, the formerly male chore of watering the livestock, which often means traveling several miles' distance from the home.

In societies where the barter system no longer provides for basic needs, earning cash has become a constant concern of rural families. If the family plot of land is mostly devoted to growing a cash crop that is to be sold in the market, it is evident that the family does not have the same quantity of food as when the entire plot was planted for the family's food supply. When the cash crop is sold (a task generally assumed by the men, again largely because of their greater mobility), many families spend as little of the earnings as possible on food. Other purchases — clothes, school supplies, household improvements, or alcohol—all compete with food for the meager cash available. The family's diet frequently deteriorates. Lacking knowledge about nutrition, families often purchase foods of little or no nutritional value. Moreover, where men have migrated to the cities or other regions to earn cash, all too frequently neither the cash nor the men get back to the families, and the women are left to fend for themselves and their children with little access to cash-earning opportunities.

〰〰

The elderly woman I was interviewing sat in the shade of a large tree outside her thatch-roofed house. She was dressed in a blue cotton dress and sandals. Her eyes were bright and gay as she talked, either sitting with her arms folded across her lap or, from time to time, fussing over a chicken that scratched the earth around us. She was a great-grand-mother who, not knowing her birthdate, thought she "might be about seventy" years old.

In that densely populated region of northwestern Kenya, many of the young people have left the land to seek employment in the larger towns. Traditionally, the women there (as elsewhere in Kenya and in the rural areas of the other countries I visited) have cultivated, processed, and cooked the family's food, and have fetched the family's water and firewood supply — in addition to bearing and raising the children. The men in that part of Kenya traditionally have been herders and warriors. Elderly family members have been held in respect and have had definite roles to play in the family hierarchy.

The woman before me was one of those elders and a leader within the community. She told of the customs of the past and of the changes taking place. She laughed at her own illiteracy — at her "ignorance," as she called it. Although she laughed often, her good-natured laughter did little to hide her disappointment with what change had brought to those around her.

"I don't really know my age, but I remember that I was married during the great war [World War I]. In those days we lived all right — happily. Things were quite different from what they are now. We got these clothes only recently. We used to wear something from banana fibers just to cover our lower parts. It was scratchy, but we were used to it. I think all the changes came when the churches came. We got our clothing, and then we said we should cover our bodies and go to school— maybe go to church.

"We had cows, goats, sheep, and hens . . . Even the chickens didn't get sick in those days. These days, more people die than used to. We had no hospitals; we were just sick, and if you knew any medicines, any herbs, you used them. There were malaria, stomachaches, and backaches. But not many used to die. They lived to be very old men and women. When you heard so-and-so was dead, everyone used to go, because that was the only funeral in a long time.

"In those days, we also used to have old women who knew herbs and helped women in childbirth and with their babies' health. In the old days, even if you had ten children you could care for them. You were happy because you had many little girls and boys to be married, as well as many grandchildren. I had nine children; three died as babies. They had diarrhea and just died. I don't know why. Now children don't die as much any more because we have doctors and hospitals nearby."

The old woman made two comments that seem contradictory: "these days more people die," and "now children don't die as much any more." In fact, these comments were simply common misinterpretations of the results of improved health care. In previous generations, the infant mortality rate was extremely high; those who reached old age were few. Thus there were in fact fewer adult deaths — for there were fewer adults to die. Now children survive and reach adulthood. There are more older people and thus more funerals to go to, as she rightly pointed out.

"What we need in this village is teachers to teach women handicrafts and sewing and agricultural skills. We have organized a women's group. I am one of the leaders. We are saving up for a building to meet in. All women are trying to earn money, and we want to have a building for our meetings. It will be called the 'adult education building' — with rooms for handicrafts, literacy, and other things.

"We also want our children to be educated — so we can have good leaders to keep our country good. I think now it is best to have only four children — so you can take care of them.

"It is better to educate a girl than a boy, although one should educate both. Girls are better. They help a lot. See this house? My daughters built it for me. If you don't have any daughters, who will build for you? The boys will marry and take care of their wives — that's all. They don't care about mothers. For example, if my son gets married, the daughter-in-law will say, 'Let's take our mothers to live with us.' The son will say, 'No, we will just have our own family and do our own things.' So you are left alone. What do you do?"

This concern about increasing disrespect for the elderly was echoed wherever I went. In Tunisia, for example, a young woman told me that older members of the family were no longer welcome within the new-style nuclear family — that "young couples want to live alone."

But the elderly Kenyan villager who talked to me had little notion of how widespread the problem actually is. She continued, saying, "And people don't respect each other like before. Since our children have gone to different schools, we see them changing. They don't respect us much anymore."

Other elderly women who had gathered around us nodded their agreement. They, too, it seemed, believed it important to educate children, but at the same time felt threatened by what becomes of educated youth. The great-grandmother summed up her disappointment with the changes she perceived:

"These days there is no trust. Men have defeated us. They don't listen; they have big heads. Before, we mixed with each other—men and women. There were no differences between us. We trusted one another,

21

but now men are not straightforward. These are the changes taking place."

In another province of Kenya, not far from the home of the great-grandmother, a nineteen-year-old student told me about her family's experience with the new needs of changing times. This young woman was of rural origin but of the generation that had benefited from educational opportunities. She said she had attended school until the age of sixteen, and that now she was participating in a six-month child-care course in preparation for employment in a nursery.

We talked in the training center once the day's lessons had been completed. The room was cold and growing even colder and dimmer as the sun set behind the hills. Dressed in a cotton dress, a heavy woolen sweater, and a kerchief tied neatly around her head, the young woman fidgeted with her hands as we talked. Her face expressed eagerness to tell about her family's life and her own plans.

"My mother has eleven children. She is my father's only wife. She works in the fields and grows the food we eat. She plants cabbage, spinach, and corn. She works very hard, but with so many children it is difficult to get enough food or money. All of my sisters and brothers go to school. One is already a teacher, and that is why I am trying to learn a profession. If I can get enough schooling, I can serve the country and my own family. I can also manage to have a life for myself. That is why I came to this school. We have a big family, and I have to help.

"My life is very different from my mother's. She just stayed in the family until she married. Life is much more difficult now because every-body is dependent on money. Long ago, money was unheard of. No one needed money. But now you can't even get food without cash. Times are very difficult. That is why the towns are creating day-care centers — so women can work and have their own lives. I have to work, for without it I will not have enough money for today's life.

"These are the problems I face and try to think about. How shall I manage to pick up this life so that I can live a better one? You know, we people of Kenya like to serve our parents when they are still alive — to help the family. But first, women have to get an education. Then if you get a large family and don't know how to feed it — if you don't have enough money for food — you can find work and get some cash. That's what I will teach my children: 'Get an education first.' "

This young woman's sense of responsibility toward her family seemed clearly tied to the growing economic difficulties facing rural families. As she sought to improve her own situation, however, she nonetheless wondered whether her new life-style would be accepted by her future husband. Her married friends were having difficulties with their husbands, and she was worried about the possibility of "getting a husband who is not kind." Her first priority, however, was to learn a profession so that she could help not only her family, but others as well.

"If I had a chance to go to the university, I would learn more about health education. I could help women that way. If I were in a position of authority, I would really try to educate women. Right now, girls are left

behind in education. It costs money, and parents think it is more important to educate boys. But I think that if people are intelligent, there is no
difference. Girls and boys should be educated the same. I would make
rules and teach women who are not educated and who have never been
to school. They, too, must understand what today's problems are. If I
have any spare time, I want to learn new things. I would like to learn how
to manage my life, my future life, and have enough say in things so that
my husband and I could understand each other and share life with our
family. And I would change the laws so that men would understand
women and their needs and not beat them as they do.

"I only hope that I will have a mature husband who will understand
and discuss things with me."

In my conversations with women in other countries, too, I was to
hear repeatedly of this desire for better understanding between men
and women. It was expressed in many ways: "Men don't consider us
human beings," or "Men just leave us and take other women in the
towns," or "We are left behind with our ignorance." These problems,
women agreed, are among those brought by the "new times."

The changes most often mentioned by rural women I interviewed as
characterizing the "new times" were increasing dependence on cash and
the newly available educational opportunities. The first of these factors
makes "life more difficult"; the second offers to their children advantages that were not available to previous generations. Improvements
such as a better water supply, health care, transportation, and electricity
were mentioned only rarely. The women were concerned mostly with
the negative elements of change: lack of land, dependence on cash,
alcoholism, and the changing attitudes of men. This was not just evidence that "good news is not news"; in many instances, serious "second
generation" problems have stymied the "first generation" benefits.

Most developing countries have, for example, spent vast sums on
their infrastructure in the last generation. They have provided health
services to rural areas; they have built schools and meeting halls; they
have taken electricity to remote villages. Yet these services often remain
inaccessible to those who live in rural areas, as they do not have the cash
needed to benefit from such amenities. Although government medical
services theoretically are free, that is not always the case. In one nation's
free clinic, for example, I witnessed a doctor asking for money from a
peasant woman who had no means of meeting his demands. Often one
must at the very least "purchase" the medicines needed.

The record of development's *mixed* results—positive and negative
—is a long one. Roads have opened up rural areas to bus services and to
trucking for the transportation of produce. But one must pay for a bus
ride and for transporting goods to market. And, as some women mentioned, the roads only serve to take the men away from the village and "to
leave us behind." The earnings of migrant men are mostly spent where
the men live and work; often, only a small percentage of these earnings is
sent back to the village.

Electricity, too, is rarely provided free of charge; few peasants benefit from the availability of electrical services, which are too costly for their incomes. The town hall or the school may have electricity, but few homes are lighted by anything more than a candle or a kerosene lamp.

While the availability of education is also an obvious gain, if children are to attend school they must dress "properly," wear shoes, and buy notebooks and pencils.

The need for cash is so pervasive and acute that it has also changed attitudes about the relative value of specific types of work. In the past, neither men nor women were paid for performing traditional family duties. Today the availability of work for money is a critical issue because some family needs can only be met with cash. Unpaid traditional roles no longer evoke respect, and women — who frequently have assumed an even larger share of these traditional family tasks — consequently have seen their authority erode within the family.

At the same time, many of the women I talked with — particularly the younger ones — are beginning to voice their needs. They want to participate in, and actively contribute to, the changing world around them. They want to be part of the decisions made concerning them; they want to choose their own husbands; they want more say in how the family's limited cash is to be spent. Nearly every woman with whom I spoke wanted her children to go as far in school as possible — expecting that an education would assure their ability to earn a decent living: "I will do *anything* to get an education for my children."

A young Sri Lankan woman expressed her awareness of new needs and opportunities as we sat and talked on the steps of a cooperative farm in Polgahawela District late one morning. She was a Buddhist and twenty-two years old. The cooperative farm of which she was a member was formed under the land reform policy of Sri Lanka. Large, privately owned estates were nationalized and organized into cooperative settlements to which many young people were attracted. Having no land themselves and facing a growing unemployment problem, they chose to settle on the farms, which offered security and companionship. The Polgahawela settlement I visited is actually *managed* by young people. They receive a small weekly wage and divide up the profits at the end of the year. The cooperative's land is covered with coconut palms and banana trees. We could hear goats and sheep in the distance.

Like most women in Sri Lanka, the young woman I spoke with had benefited from the nation's free educational system. She had attended school until the age of eighteen. She was dressed in Western style, in a skirt and blouse, with her long, dark hair pulled to one side in a single braid. She said she was the eldest of nine children and had felt that it was her duty to stop schooling and earn a living.

Like the child-care student in Kenya, this young Sri Lankan is of the new generation that has witnessed a changing economic situation. Thousands of miles from each other, with enormous cultural differences separating them, the two young women articulated the same needs and a similar sense of the individual's responsibility for family and country.

"My mother's generation did not have all the opportunities we have. They did not have education, health services, or the transportation systems that exist now. But economically, they were better off. The income they got was sufficient to meet all their needs. At the moment, the high cost of living makes life difficult. They find it difficult to have a happy life.

"Today young people have the opportunity to show their capabilities in sports and cultural activities — even in social and public affairs. Earlier generations did not allow girls to leave the home and attend public meetings. Now we have that opportunity. Even without the consent of our parents, we take part in social and public affairs or in political matters.

"That is why I wanted to come and join this cooperative. When I live at home, I have no freedom. Wherever I go, I have to be accompanied by a brother and I have to return home early. I am questioned all the time. There is no freedom. But here I can earn my living and have some freedom to move about and make choices about participation in after-work activities.

"Of course, my parents didn't want me to come here. They refused at first. They were concerned about letting a daughter come to a place like this, but the second time I asked — or rather, insisted — they gave their consent.

"You see, my father is a farmer. My parents lived from the land, but when my grandfather died, the land was distributed among his sons. Now my parents' portion is very small. It is not sufficient for them to exist on. They continue to work the land and to search for other jobs.

"I want my children to have a firmer footing—not to have this type of life. They must learn a profession and have a better job than mine. Women in Sri Lanka need employment. They should all have jobs. They must be taught skills so that they can earn a bit for their families.

"I will have only two children: When you have more than two, you have all sorts of problems and expenses to worry about. For me, I hope to lead a happy, quiet, honest life that will be useful to my country — that will help the country's development."

This young woman's family was caught in a predicament common to many families in the rural areas of developing countries; the land they own, subdivided among the members of their larger families, is no longer sufficient for their support. In this young woman's opinion, the mobility to learn and earn are essential to improving her family's, and her own, welfare. Her allusions to a still larger social responsibility—the notion of "helping the country" that I heard again and again from younger women interviewed in other countries — seemed a reflection not only of schooling, but also of communications campaigns to increase public awareness of national development needs and objectives.

For many of the older women I interviewed, education and training opportunities were not accessible, and the possibility of adequate self-support was slim. These women want to provide their children with better opportunities than they have, and they bitterly resent the necessity of taking children out of school to help in the struggle for the family's survival.

One such woman was Lucia — fifty-five years old, illiterate, and extremely poor. The town in which she lives is in the rich El Bahio region of central Mexico. The town is surrounded by huge farms owned by corporate firms. The men of the region find only seasonal work here because the farms are highly mechanized. Throughout this region, production of export crops has displaced farming for domestic consumption, and the nutritional problems of the area are acute. A young doctor told me that 90 per cent of the population suffers from nutritional deficiencies. Anemia is very common among women.

Lucia is landless and has no remunerable skills. She was dressed in ragged clothes and broken plastic sandals. Her eyes were those of a person who expects nothing but hardship in the years still ahead. Her skin was dark, and she covered her head and shoulders with a worn, green shawl. She did not look up at the start of our conversation, keeping her head bowed, as if she considered herself unworthy to be there.

She was visiting the health center because her daughter had just had her ninth child by caesarean birth. The child had died, but the grandmother was not sad, saying, "How would her husband ever feed another mouth when he earns only 25 pesos [U.S. $1.18] per day?" As we talked, Lucia began to relax a little, to look at me occasionally, and to speak candidly about her life.

"I am fifty-five years old, and those years have not been good. I didn't even have shoes or many clothes. I was very, very poor. Every night I had to wash my clothes and then put them on again in the morning. I didn't have anything at all, just the fifteen children. But only seven of my children are still living. The other eight died when they were babies. I think it was because of the hunger. I was very weak while nursing them because we never had enough to eat. All we had was beans, beans, and more beans. Yes, it was the hunger that took the babies. My husband was a laborer, but my mother-in-law kept the money. My husband was cruel with me. He beat me and screamed at me. He did many, many bad things. When he died, I sent the children to work as cattle herders. The owner of the cattle gives us some food. They eat better now."

Many women I met during my travels complained of being beaten regularly, and from Lucia I learned that wife beating is a common occurrence in her village as well. She told me that the village priest has little influence in controlling the violence of the men of his parish.

"My husband used to drink; that is why he would beat me. Both he and his mother would drink. This is the big problem here: men spend all the money they have on liquor. We have so much poverty and drunkenness. It makes me sad because I remember the time when it was like that for me."

When I asked Lucia what positive changes had occurred in her village during her lifetime, she replied:

"Before, women were very, very stupid. They didn't realize what life was because they didn't have any education or anything. But now women are beginning to work and go to school; they are beginning to know many things and are becoming better. They can decide what *they* want to do, as it should be. My daughter just had her tubes tied after she had a caesarean. I am happy about this, because they are very poor and I don't like my daughter to suffer.

"I hoped that my children would finish primary school. The fifteen-year-old wanted to continue, but I could not afford the books and supplies he needed. He tries to find work and help me, but there is no work around here. He gives me what he earns, and I try to find work washing laundry. This is all we have."

Toward the end of our conversation, Lucia, twisting her dark rough hands as she spoke, told me that her life did not make much sense to her. With a flash of bitterness, she added: "I don't understand why God put me here."

In Tunisia, I was told a more encouraging story — one of hope and courage — by a woman whose opportunities had been almost as limited as those of Lucia. She was a Bedouin, a member of one of the thousands of families who follow nomadic routes from south to north and back again, according to the seasons. They herd the livestock of others and work on olive plantations at harvest time, eking out a living as they move from region to region — just as their ancestors have done for centuries before them.

Like Lucia, this Bedouin woman had never attended school; her feelings of self-worth seemed rooted in the improved status of women in Tunisia, which is due to enlightened legal codes that have been in effect for over twenty years. She was dressed in a worn, faded *meliah* — the long piece of material that is wrapped and draped around the body to make a dress, usually held together with great, silver, buckle-like brooches. But this woman owned no brooch. Her tattered dress was held by safety pins. She had been working in the field across the road from a rural health center on the road to Sfax. With an interpreter, I had been interviewing several women, and she had watched us from afar; at one point she had dared to approach us to ask what we were doing. Guessing what her reply would be, I asked if she would like to talk with us. She smiled, and we crossed the road to sit in the field where she worked. Interrupted now and then by the bleating of sheep, she told her story.

"I was given in marriage at age thirteen. I hadn't even reached puberty. My father was dead, so my uncle arranged the marriage with a neighbor. Now it is better; there is a law that says girls mustn't marry before the age of seventeen. That is good. You know, I hadn't had my period when I married. A month later it came—and a month after that I was pregnant. I had five children — three girls and two boys — but one daughter was stillborn.

"My children go to school, and I want them, both sons and daughters, to go as far as their ability lets them. I want them to have a good future, a profession, a happy life. I don't want them working in the fields, picking up straws and leftovers as I do. I would like so much to have gone to school. I would like to have opened my mind. I would have taught other people about things. I want to know everything — everything you can learn if you have an education. I won't let my daughters marry earlier than seventeen. I want them to have time to finish their studies, prepare their trousseau, and prepare themselves for marriage.

"Men are much better these days than they were before. They respect women more. Now they learn things, they are more understanding, they understand the rights of men and of women, too. And now a man can no longer divorce a wife he tires of. Before, a woman could be divorced, beaten, and poorly treated. That kind of thing doesn't exist anymore, thanks to President Bourguiba. Thanks to him and the laws, women are much better off today.

"We have family planning now, and you can take better care of your children. That, too, is different. You can't imagine how many things I tried to swallow to prevent myself from having more children. I even used to eat mothballs, thinking that would help. I am only thirty-six years old, and I have planned my family now for five years. I have a loop. I don't want any more children. Life is too difficult." She glanced away for a moment, pausing, and then added, with great seriousness: "Before the new laws, all women lived the lives of beasts."

One hot and dusty afternoon, I spent several hours in the home of two Moslem women — a young woman of twenty-seven and her sixty-five-year-old mother — in Port Sudan on the Red Sea. The daughter had been married at seventeen and now had four children. She had always lived in this urban area, where she had attended school for nine years. She cradled her youngest child in her arms while a three-year-old slept in the crib between us. She was a heavy-set woman, dressed in a wide, smock-like summer dress. Her hair was pulled back in a knot behind her neck. Her husband, whom she had been permitted to meet before her marriage, was a teacher in Port Sudan.

"Mother's life was, and is, very different from my own. She couldn't go out or talk to any men other than her husband. She never even went out into the street with him. She just stays home all the time; that is her life. But I go to market; I go out with my husband; we may even go to a movie. My husband does not mind. Sometimes I don't even put on my *tow* [the semi-transparent veil used to cover the shoulders, head and body]. Mother would never go outside without a full veil covering her face and hair.

"These changes are all due to education. Before, women did not go to school. They did not know their husbands. They never saw them until the wedding night, once they were already married. But here in Sudan, women don't have as much access to education as men. It is better for boys — much better. I want my children to have more education than I did; then they will be different from me, just as I am different from my mother. The main thing is education. Schools are very important for girls.

"A girl and a boy must be equal. A woman must work in all areas — doctor, teacher, anything. Any work a man can do, a woman can do also . Unfortunately, though, so far these changes have been more for educated people than for the poor."

I interrupted to ask her whether she thought that any laws should be changed in Sudan to help women. Her answer, after a long pause, revealed great caution:

"That question should be left for a time. Later there will be progress, perhaps, but for the time being, no laws will be changed. I hope that Sudan will improve, just like the developed countries. This is my only wish. I don't think Sudan is bad now, but I hope for development."

When we left the house later that afternoon, the interpreter, a young social worker, told me: "Sudanese women do not like to discuss law or politics." It was a hint meant to be a helpful warning. The young wife perceived her life to be very different from that of her mother, yet she was not yet accustomed to expressing her own views — or was deliberately reluctant to do so. Her response was not unique among the Sudanese women with whom I spoke. Legal equality with men is part of the country's laws, but it is seldom enforced and is often blurred by contradictory practices. Aware of the demands of tradition and customs — and understandably apprehensive about possible retaliation — few women dare to speak about the inadequate enforcement of laws.

Fathia Al Assal, whom I interviewed in Egypt, certainly is not a woman who fears to voice her opinions. Her story is one of growing awareness and of a persistent will to achieve. Despite little formal education, Fathia is, at forty-four, a well-known writer and playwright. She is active in women's groups and possesses a strong political consciousness. She explained with humor that she is the daughter of a businessman who wed twenty women in the course of his life.

"He never kept more than four wives at a time. That is the law's limit. In all, he sired fifteen children—seven from my mother and eight from other wives. He married my mother when she was only fourteen. She was his first wife. She did not see him before the wedding. She was illiterate and had been raised traditionally. My father stayed with my mother throughout his other marriages. The last marriage was a marriage of love, and it was with the last woman that he had seven other children."

Fathia hesitated a moment, and then recounted a childhood experience that had strongly affected her own views. When her father had married a second woman without telling her, Fathia's mother insisted on a divorce. But her own family came to call on her. Fathia's grandmother told her mother:

"Stay where you are. You have no choice. You have only two alternatives, because you can't provide for yourself or your children. Either you stay with this man as his wife and bring up his children, or you come back with me and leave the children with their father."

The economic predicament, Fathia noted, had been evident to her even then. Her mother was trapped by it and had to stay where she was. Fathia told me that she herself had very little schooling—only one year:

"My father was dead set against educating girls — including his daughters. He educated his sons very well, but he kept his daughters from school the moment they began to develop signs of adolescence. I think he was afraid that they might have inherited his sins — that they might want to run around as he did. I think he had a deep sense of guilt about the way he treated his women.

"I managed to learn how to read and write in the year I stayed in school. Later I read avidly the books in my father's library. I read whatever I could find. If purchases were wrapped in newspaper, I would read the newspaper. All the time I had a motive: to be different from my mother. I loved her, but I was under the impression that something was lacking in her. My father always wanted to learn, to acquire new knowledge. My mother didn't.

"I was engaged once to an army officer. But he started to argue with me about reading books. He believed that reading books would corrupt the mind of a woman. I broke the engagement. I knew that I had no education and thus no means for a decent job, but I had reached the stage where I would have preferred to work in a shop rather than stay at home, as a dependent. But my father of course would not let me work in a shop. It was then that I met my husband, and he encouraged me. He made me read political theory and socialist thought. I was changed by the contact with this man who encouraged me to learn more and to do with my life what I could.

"I started a school for illiterate women — working women, sales girls, and very poor women — and I taught them how to read. As I was doing so, I noticed that at certain times they completely lost interest in what we were doing because the radio was broadcasting a serial play. They lost all interest the moment they heard the opening musical theme. I said to myself, if art is that effective, why not use it to influence and educate these women? That very same night I wrote — or made an attempt to write — my first play. It was a comical play about medical prescriptions. You see, our women are ignorant and superstitious. My play taught them the difference between witchcraft and real medicine, and it was meant to be educational. I try to give the notion to women that they must take hold of their lives by economic independence. I do this in all my plays."

Fathia told me of her commitment to help and educate the women who have had little opportunity to participate in life outside the immediate family. Her expression hardened when she began to tell of the factors that keep women tied to traditional roles:

"We have a problem with our religious leaders. They are the enemies of women. They are the enemies of women simply because they are the enemies of progress. If there is no progress, they keep their influence and continue as representatives of a privileged class. Progress, you see, among other things, means the equality between a man and a woman. The ideal relationship is one in which there is no sense of possession.

"The emancipation of women is only part and parcel of the emancipation of society as a whole. I don't find the emancipation of women (if it is possible) sufficient in itself. I would remove all kinds of oppression, whether of men or women or social classes. But women must learn theory if they are to advance."

Fathia paused a moment and then added:

"Do you know what women lack most? The knowledge, the deep-rooted knowledge and conviction, that they are *human beings.*"

# 3

WOMEN WITHIN THE FAMILY

# "We are like trees growing in the shade"

## WOMEN WITHIN THE FAMILY

At a training center for young rural women some forty miles from Sfax, Tunisia, I talked with an eighteen-year-old girl named Zohra who was attending a six-month course to learn an income-earning skill. Because many Tunisian families still do not allow their daughters out of the home before marriage, the center teaches skills that can be practiced within the home. Prior to coming here, Zohra had left her home only a few times — to attend weddings or for occasional visits to the cemetery. After a few months of training in weaving rugs, sewing, and knitting, she was to return to her father's house. Once she had acquired a skill, she explained, she would be a more useful daughter and, eventually, a more desirable bride.

She told me that she was born in a rural area, but that her family, which was poor and landless, had moved to the outskirts of Sfax, where her father and brothers could find occasional employment. As we sat in the empty refectory of the training center, Zohra told me about her family.

"I went to school for three years, but since I was the eldest of the family of seven children, my mother counted on me to help with the housework and cooking. With all the schoolwork and housework and the severity of the schoolmaster, I got discouraged. One time he gave me a thousand lines to copy. When I came back to the house, all I could think about was the thousand lines. I lost my head worrying about the two responsibilities. I never went back to school. I regret it now. I am unable to do anything because of my lack of education. I am unhappy to be in this situation. I am always enclosed in what others call my ignorance.

"My father won't let me out of the house at all; he won't let me cross the threshold of our house except to come here to learn a skill. My brother did not want me to come here. He was totally against it. He is very strict. But my mother had heard that this center is very isolated and that I would risk nothing here — that I would be kept in security — and she explained that to my father. Despite my brother's opposition, my father was finally persuaded. He said I could come here so I could learn how to work, since, he said, 'What will I do with you if you don't know how to earn a living?'

33

"I have never been anywhere. I can't go out or have fun. I live just outside Sfax, you know, but I have never visited the city. I left my father's home, which is the first prison, to come to this isolated village. It is the second prison. When I finish I will return to prison number one — and from there, if it ever happens that I marry, I will go into prison three — my husband's home. I can only hope I will get a husband who will understand me and be willing to talk with me. But I don't know what fate holds in store for me."

Zohra's words echoed those of many women I met during my trip. They point out important dimensions of the family dilemma in a rapidly changing society: the fragility of interpersonal relationships within the family and the absence of communication among its members at a time when roles are being questioned constantly. Where the choice of marriage partners is made by families rather than the individuals concerned, it cannot be assumed that the husband and wife talk things over or plan together, or that there is any intimacy or even a sense of partnership between them. Countless times I was told that couples rarely talk with each other. There is "women's talk" and "men's talk," but little "together" talk.

In many cultures the notion of male dominance — of man as woman's "god," protector, and provider — and the notion of women as passive, submissive, and chaste have been the predominant images for centuries. In many cases, customary practices have been based on a pecking order that has not always been conducive to the well-being and personal development of those lower down the status line. Yet traditional family structures did provide family members with clearly defined roles and responsibilities within which one could maneuver and earn recognition. Decisions were reached according to accepted procedures and were not questioned. Today those patterns — and consequently, individual self-perceptions — are going through a period of rapid transformation. All family members — men, women, and children, whether old, young, or middle-aged — are affected by the economic and social changes taking place. Each individual sees his or her role challenged. Family members witness, and are disturbed by, the changes they see in each other, and this reinforces their sense of insecurity. Most members of rural families do not have the benefit of an education or the skills to enable them to cope with a barrage of new demands. Men may be able to find work opportunities locally or by migration to other areas. Women can only *try* to adjust as best they can to the new situation and to the new roles delegated to them.

Throughout my talks with women, I constantly heard of the new roles they were assuming, of their new-found vulnerabilities and needs, and of their changing perceptions both of the value of what they do at present and what they might do in the future. Replies to one question asked of each woman in all six countries revealed the prevalence of a strong wish to emerge from the very limited roles to which they were bound by tradition. The question I asked was simple: "Was there any time in your life, as a child or even now, when you said to yourself, 'I wish I had been born a boy'?" The majority of the uneducated women replied: "Yes—I could then have studied and learned," or "I could have gone out of the house and seen other things," or "I could have helped my country." The reasons they gave clearly had nothing to do with wishing to be males per se, but simply denoted their desire to be able to participate in society as do the males around them. One young woman who had been abandoned by her husband remarked, "I would like to be a man so I could take care of my wife and family better than we are living now."

Early one warm morning I walked along the shaded streets of Colombo, Sri Lanka, on my way to the home of a well-known and respected political scientist, Kumari Jayawardene. Our discussion took place in her study, a porch-like structure that was a breezy haven in the humid city. Dr. Jayawardene divides her time between research, writing, and lecturing on political and economic issues relating to women. Her husband is a prominent Sri Lankan economist. For two hours we talked mainly about the status of women within the family and within society—its origins and its political implications.

I asked Dr. Jayawardene if the worldwide issue of equality for women had had an influence on the women of her country and on the Sri Lankan family. The question seemed to reach deep into her own concerns:

"I think that at some point one has to ask the question, 'Is the family going to survive in future society?' This question has not been debated at all. I don't say that mutual respect between marriage partners will necessitate the destruction of the family, but it will bring into question the family unit as it operates today. From what I see, the family is very restraining, and it is ultimately the thing that oppresses a woman. Accepting the family as a unit as it exists today in our society means accepting the relegation of women to doing things that I consider to be a hindrance to their personal lives from the beginning. Women's whole lives are devoted to other people's personal problems. They are told that society, politics, and economics, for example, are men's concerns. But the family must continue, so someone has to do that — has to do the 'womanly tasks.' Until you 'socialize,' in a sense, the cooking and the washing and the major problems with which the woman is burdened — until some solution is found, and it has to be a *social* solution — she will continue to live in this isolated family, in which, I think, her oppression is perpetrated. And even if you give her economic 'independence' without changing the way things are done at the level of the family unit, then a woman is doubly oppressed: she is made to work outside the home and is enslaved within it at the same time.

"Also, the women's question still causes some emotional reactions— even among men who take a progressive stance on any other issue. Even among my male colleagues who agree with me on just about everything else, I find some who have a mental and emotional block on the women's issue. Some of them take it personally. They themselves have wives —

housewives and slaves — so they have to justify it by saying, 'It is our tradition,' or 'Women's liberation is some mad Western idea that has nothing to do with us.' That element is *definitely* there. I suppose it is the psychology of one group oppressing another and then having to rationalize and justify it."

I asked Dr. Jayawardene about the relationship of Buddhism — Sri Lanka's predominant religion — to the roles assumed by men and women within the family.

"I don't agree that in Buddhist countries women have more freedom. Certainly Buddhism was a step forward in its time, but now it has become institutionalized — just another religion that people use for their own purposes. I think it is used *against* women because all the Buddhas said that society must be patriarchal. True, there were times when women were given a bit more freedom — but patriarchy continues.

"Actually, you know, women really don't *understand* that they are exploited. When I talk with women's groups I realize this. One day an old woman spoke up and said that she agreed with everything I had said about the situation of women, but that women 'must still have fear and shame, for such are their qualities.' That's an expression here in Sri Lanka. 'Fear,' meaning submissiveness, and 'shame,' meaning modesty. Submissiveness and modesty, she said, women must have.

"For example, men eat first in our society. They don't eat with the women. The women cook. The men sit. The women serve. The women stand while the men eat, and, after that, if there's anything left, the women eat. Males — fathers and sons and male guests — are always served first. As a result, the women are often undernourished, as are the girls of the family.

"One of the major problems is that women feel that they are inferior — that they can't be like men, that their brains are not as good, that they are not as educated. Timidity is a problem, fear of speaking up. But once you make women aware that they have the same brain as a man and can have the same education, you give them back their self-confidence."

Dr. Jayawardene added that over a period of years she had observed the emergence of a new attitude among young Sri Lankan women — a new self-confidence about marriage and the choice of a marriage partner. Greater economic independence is an obvious explanation of this trend: young women who work feel more free to plan their own lives.

"Today parents want their daughters to work. They want them to be chaste, yes — 'a woman's most precious possession is her virginity' — and they want them to follow all the traditional customs. But they do want them to work. This financial independence sometimes permits the daughters to choose their own husbands. So now choosing a husband is a new concept — a new hope.

"There was a time, though, when *all* marriages were arranged by the family. The children were introduced, and then they had to go out together a bit. It was an arrangement whereby parents chose the family into which they wished their daughter to marry."

Dr. Jayawardene explained that she had been fortunate — that her own family, especially her father, had espoused the idea of the full participation of women in society. As she reminisced about her family, she smiled, saying:

"I was an only child, and a *girl*. In a Sri Lankan family, that is a sad thing for a father. Right in front of me people would say to my father, 'What a pity you did not have a son.'

"I don't know for what reason, but I think my father always believed that women should be emancipated. For example, he was against the dowry. He even brought a motion against the dowry system in parliament in 1936. But the motion was defeated. He had modern ideas, and he always pushed me on. He treated me as if I were a boy. He pushed me on from one class to another, and I would say, 'Oh, that's enough. I'm a mere girl. How can I pass that examination?' But he would say, 'Go on, go on.' He'd take me somewhere and say, 'This is my daughter. She's in school and she's done this and that,' and I would feel embarrassed and ashamed. My father influenced me very much."

In my talks with women I interviewed, I found this last point repeated with surprising frequency. Especially in the cases of upper-class women, it was often the father rather than the mother who supported a daughter's desire for a nontraditional role. In a sense this is not very surprising, since upper-class men are usually well educated and — given their financial security — risk very little when they do not conform to accepted traditional attitudes; their wives, on the other hand, are less inclined to question the status quo, since they often are expected to do nothing *but* conform. As Kumari Jayawardene herself commented, she was at first uncomfortable and "embarrassed" by her father's constant effort to push her out of the traditional role expected of a Sri Lankan girl.*

But upper-class women were by no means the only ones to cite a strong paternal influence on their lives. Whenever I asked women to tell me who had influenced them most in childhood—their mothers or their fathers — their answer, regardless of social class, almost invariably was "my father." Most women said that their mothers had taught them "how to behave" and "how to care for the house and the children," but that it had been their fathers who had either encouraged them to participate in outside activities or, on the contrary, had forbidden them to do so. In both the positive and negative cases, however, the father had been the more important influence. For example, a poor peasant woman in Mexico who had received encouragement from her father and husband told me she was able to participate in community activities more than were her friends. Conversely, women of the upper classes who had been limited to traditional roles had been discouraged from doing so by their fathers or, later, by their husbands. Given the degree of male dominance that permeates the cultures of the countries I visited, this is not really very surprising. What it does usefully clarify, however, is that women's relative personal "underdevelopment" and low status in the family often prevent them from playing an important role in guiding the life choices of their children — girls as well as boys.

---

*Often, regardless of the economic and social standing of their families, the women who clearly had benefited from a father's support of their educational and other endeavors were daughters of parents who had no sons. This pattern has been noted by other observers in other countries (including the United States), and its implications merit more attention.

Only in a few cases did I find that the mother had played a vital role in encouraging a female child to seek to develop her abilities beyond the bounds of roles circumscribed by tradition. One woman I interviewed in Villagran, in rural Mexico, told me:

"My father didn't want my sisters and me to go to school, but my mother influenced him and we did go. Once my father threatened us. He warned us not to go to school. My mother came out and said, 'My children are going back to school.' "

In Cairo, Nawal Es Saadawi, a medical doctor and author, told me:

"My mother was very intelligent, and she was frustrated because she had lost her career because of marriage. She was always warning, 'I lost my career so don't lose yours.' "

Even among the educated women I interviewed, however, this was an atypical pattern. Only in a very few cases had the women's mothers strongly encouraged their personal development beyond traditional roles.

In Juba, Sudan, a well-educated young woman, Victoria Yar Arol, a member of the People's Regional Assembly, told me that she was the only member of the family who had gone to school for any length of time. Her father was a tribal chief and had many wives. She thought he had fathered about twenty or thirty children, but even the sons did not continue their education. About her own education, she said:

"It was my father who wanted it. My mother was very much opposed to my education because she wanted her daughters to relieve her of the family work. I happened to be the only one who did well, so my father kept on encouraging me until I got my highest education."

After my interview with Kumari Jayawardene in Colombo, I traveled through other parts of Sri Lanka. I found, as Dr. Jayawardene had said I would, that many young Sri Lankan women (whether they were Buddhists, Hindus, or Catholics) expected their lives to be controlled—often quite unquestioningly—by the men in their families.

One young woman I interviewed in a village southeast of Colombo told me that, at twenty-two, she considers her life to be much better than her mother's had been; whereas her mother's marriage had been arranged by the family, she herself had been allowed to choose her own husband. Yet despite her feeling that she was more independent than her mother, her conversation revealed her own absolute submissiveness to her husband's authority. Married at eighteen, she had three daughters and hoped to have one more child, a son. She told me she spends her days carrying out the chores of housewifery and tending a small family garden to supplement the family diet. Although she was a small woman, slight and delicate, she conveyed an impression of strength. She seemed self-confident as she talked about her family:

"My grandmother and mother did not go to school long, and they were not allowed to choose their husbands or go out of the home. When my daughters get to the marriage age and pick out their partners, I will inquire and find out who they are. If they are all right, I will let them marry.

"I have been married for four years. It was a 'love match.' I am at the peak of my marriage. I want to have only one more child, a son. But I can't make that decision on my own; I must discuss it with my husband. I don't want too many children because of our income and the need for education. Both girls and boys should get an education today."

She was silent for a moment, and I asked if she thought women were as capable as men to be leaders if they received the same education. Her answer indicated that while she wants her daughters as well as her sons to have equal opportunities, she still totally accepts the notion of women's absolute submission to male authority:

"Men should have more power. That is the way it is: men have more power. A woman must be submissive. Peace and harmony in the family depend upon the woman. She must always listen to the man. She must give obedience and all that to the husband. Yes, men must wield authority."

In Sudan, I spoke with an educated young woman, a law student, who expressed a similar view. She was in her early twenties and was about to be married. Although she agreed with many of the "liberal" ideas of her colleagues, in practice she would accept the traditional woman's role. She believed she should always submit to her husband's wishes, even if he forbad her to continue her legal studies.

"I want to study more, and then I will marry this July. It will be difficult for me to study, but I will do my best. My husband finished the university, so I want to study also. I am interested in studying law because women are working in politics now."

I asked her whether her husband also wanted her to go on with her studies.

"Well, when I talked to him about it he didn't refuse, but I don't know what will happen after we marry. He might refuse."

Although she was interested in law and politics, this young woman seemed willing to accept the possibility that her husband might forbid her to study or to participate in activities outside the home once they married.

Such family constraints have not been part of the life of Amina Saïd, whom I interviewed in Cairo, where she is today president of a modern corporation, Egypt's largest publishing house. Even among upper-class Egyptian women, however, her story is exceptional. As the daughter of a medical doctor, she had benefited since childhood from the care of parents who were both wealthy and progressive in their outlook. She had been one of the first Egyptian women to attend a university. She chose her own husband and continued to work after marriage, thereby breaking with Egyptian family tradition.

Today she is an influential journalist, a social activist, and a proud grandmother. During our talk in her downtown Cairo office, Mrs. Saïd reflected on the changes that had taken place since the days of her youth.

Her experience again shows how a father's concern for his daughter's personal growth can be the deciding factor in overcoming those traditions that tend to hinder women's full participation in society. Commenting that she was the third child in a family of four daughters and one son, she told me that her father had educated all of them and given them their first "big push" in life:

"By the time he died, we were already full of pride, self-respect, and the belief that women are not less than men in any way—or rather, as he said to us, that 'they are not better than you.' He wanted us to be everything that men can be. He wanted to give us all the opportunities possible. He used to help us do things that were not accepted by others.

"When I entered the university and also wanted to join in social activities or sports like tennis, he even encouraged me in that. Girls didn't play tennis in those days, but my father said, 'Do it at once. It is good for your health. I am paying university fees—not only the fees for the university activities, but for sports and everything. This is your right and you go on with it. If you don't, you will be a big coward. And furthermore, I want to tell you that if *they* dismiss you from the university for practicing one of your rights, as they threatened, my present will be to send you to the best university in Europe to finish your education. But if *you* back down, admitting they are right, I will keep you at home and you will become one of the herd.'

"He used the word 'herd'—meaning all the women of the country who were not emancipated—so I was frightened. I wanted to fight for my rights. This experience really gave me courage."

Mrs. Saïd also related how her husband had encouraged her at the beginning of her career—even before they were married. She said that she had always wanted to write, but that her mother, despite her relatively progressive outlook, was not the type of woman who would accept having her daughter become a journalist.

"You see, there were no women in the press until then. I was the first one to do it. Having a daughter working in journalism was practically like having a daughter working in a striptease nightclub. Traditional families couldn't possibly think of it. It was awful. I was the first to do it, so, unfortunately, I had to do it behind my mother's back. I was engaged to my husband and he was a great help. He used to come every afternoon and take me from home, saying that he would take me to the movies. After dinner he would take me to my office so that I could work and then he would bring me back. From the very beginning he was supportive of my career and helped me a great deal."

However unique Amina Saïd's life may be in its particulars, the importance that she herself attributed to the encouragement she had received from her father (and husband) was a common point emphasized by most of the more assertive women I interviewed. Regardless of the country or social class, I found that if a woman was more competent, active, and optimistic than other women of her peer group, it was generally because she had been urged on by some supportive male in her family. If, on the other hand, she was resigned and self-deprecating, I almost invariably learned in the course of our conversation that she belonged to a family in which no woman dared question male authority.

The more extreme forms of male dominance that still characterize many societies — not only the ones I visited on this "mission" — clearly create serious problems for girl children. The full implications of such dominance need to be better understood. Certainly it is likely that it is an enormous deterrent to improving the quality of life not only of women themselves — as individuals — but also of their families and societies.

Although most women comply with what is traditionally expected of them, there are some who do revolt — despite the consequences. Changing perceptions of their own rights and needs are leading some women to defy customary roles in desperate attempts to improve their existence.

Maria Luisa is a woman I visited in an isolated Zapotec Indian village in southern Mexico. I had spent the afternoon with her — watching her grind corn kernels into mush, roll tortillas, cook them, and give one now and then to the tiny child who clutched at her skirt. Maria Luisa's sister, Anna, who lived nearby, was also expected to come that afternoon and talk with us, but we waited for her in vain. Maria Luisa spoke to me about her sister's life:

"She is in the process of breaking up with her husband. They have four children, but they didn't get married until the third child was born. Then the priest said, 'If you don't get married, I'm not baptizing your children.'

"Anna's husband wants to live like the old men used to live — having women right under his thumb — not the way it is today. Even our family is against it. They say, 'He has such old-fashioned ideas.' The woman has to be in the house. She has to confess everything to him. She can't have a thought of her own. Even that's okay. You can be jealous. You can even be a tyrant. *But you have to do your share.* You have to bring in money. The reason the family is so down on him is not because he's a tyrant, but because he doesn't fulfill his part of the marriage. She has to go out and look for food while he's gallivanting around. That's what doesn't make sense. You know — rules are rules.

"Now he's beating her even more than before because his mother is constantly filling his head with ideas. 'Anna doesn't cook good food,' she says — and things like that. He beats her up; she is black and blue on the thighs or on the back or wherever. He says he has the right to rule. You know, the male doesn't want to be made a fool of. He accuses other men of being weak. He says, 'I'm not like those men. I don't let women give orders in my house.'

"But Anna is a good wife. She works hard, and if he would let her out of the house, their family would have more money. She works hard in the field, but he doesn't even give her money for food. Granted, he doesn't really earn that much himself, but he *could.* He could take crops into town and sell them and bring back the money, but he doesn't. He feels she shouldn't have money. He works in the field, but he doesn't look for other work. So he gets very little. He doesn't want to sell much, and there is not enough money to feed the family, so Anna has to sell things or borrow five pesos here and there. Then he gets enraged and blames her for not managing. And this is where the mother-in-law comes in. The old woman thinks Anna can make do with even less. But if there's no money, you can't buy food. If there's no money, you can't buy tomatoes. And our new generation knows that children have to have their food."

Maria Luisa told me that her sister now wanted to leave — to go to Mexico City to find work. She wondered how Anna was going to manage:

"She's so nervous all the time; she needs a rest. But she's going to leave her husband and leave the children with him and take the baby. She wants to go someplace else. She's not going to go back to him. She said, 'I don't have to. I can't bear this. Who else would put up with him as long as I have?' "

Had she lived a generation before, Anna would not have had the option of leaving her husband, her children, and her village to seek work elsewhere. But her "option" is a choice of last resort. She will become one of the thousands of peasant women who migrate to the cities each year— alone, illiterate, untrained in any income-earning skill, totally unfamiliar with the world beyond the village, and highly vulnerable to new, though different, threats to their day-to-day existence.

In Kenya, traditions of cooperative living that have evolved from a family structure based on tribal life and polygamy have aided rural women today in adapting to the "more difficult times" brought by rapid economic change. A long tradition of cooperative modes of work has helped to strengthen the women's self-help movement about which I heard in villages throughout Kenya. In Machakos, a large town in central Kenya, I met with a group of women who had formed a cooperative to aid the destitute women of the area. The leader of the Machakos women's cooperative, a large, tall woman of fifty-four, is a successful businesswoman who owns and rents out several houses and has opened both a grocery store and a hardware shop. She had no children of her own, but had adopted one of her sister's sons. She told me that this boy has married two women, and she proudly announced that she has ten grandchildren.

She said she had seen the difficulties of women's lives increase since her mother's time. She noted, however, that as the family's structure has been weakened by the demands of new patterns of economic activity and changing values, some women have been able to turn to each other for help:

"Most women don't rely on their husbands now. If they get some money, well and good; and if they don't, they just try to get money for themselves — selling vegetables or making and selling handicrafts.

"Life is very difficult these days, and men are paying less attention to their wives. You see, men have wrongly just taken advantage of having more money. Instead of using money properly, to improve the lives of their families, they spend it on all the 'facilities' available at hotels. Instead of spending nights in their own homes, they fight at home and seek women outside—in the hotels. Many men cheat on their wives now because they are employed and have money. A husband can say, 'I have been sent as a driver to Nairobi' (or elsewhere), when he actually spends the money on girls.

"So women are fed up. They think now that relying on a man can be a problem. They say, 'We should try to do something ourselves. Then, whether we get something from our men or not, we still will be able to raise our children properly.' The problem that many women face is that they must become self-supporting. They either have no support from their husbands at all, or very little. And there is no law to protect them.

"But women *are* trying to do something for themselves, and if they had the capital they could establish businesses to help them make money. The main problem here is the money problem. Many women are alone. They need to earn for their families."

Thus once again I heard about the "money problem" and about the struggle of women who are the sole support of their children. As families strive to adapt to the needs of the changing times, and as traditions and relationships are transformed, many women are left behind, without skills and with little mobility. And, as they themselves say, "men hold the key" to their fate. The support and encouragement of the men who govern their lives seem to be critical to women's advancement and, ultimately, to their participation in the development process itself.

The successful Machakos businesswoman shared with me her perception of yet another psychological toll of traditional status differences between men and women within the family:

"Women feel very hurt because they think their men don't recognize them as human beings. They are unhappy because of this inequality. I am lucky; my husband is good. He never took another wife. We are still together." She added a thought that I was to hear repeatedly in conversations with other women: "My wish would be that men and women could live as two equal people."

# 4

A LEGACY OF SOCIAL CONSTRAINTS

# "But it is still a privilege to be born a man"

## A LEGACY OF SOCIAL CONSTRAINTS

National laws defining women's status are at best an incomplete guide to assessing the situation of women in any country, and the developing countries I visited are no exception. Wide gaps exist between laws, women's knowledge and understanding of them, and enforcement of the law by authorities. These gaps are especially evident in rural areas, where women lack the most basic information about their legal rights.

Many of the rural women with whom I spoke knew nothing about the rights of divorced women or widows — or of children born out of wedlock. Moreover, their perceptions of "women's status" were still affected by numerous practices — often based on taboos, superstitions, religious beliefs, or even misinterpretations of religious tenets — that continue to have a stunting effect on their personal development, assertiveness, and participation in the life around them. In many cultures, centuries-old customs and practices continue to support common perceptions of women as weak, inferior — even unable to resist temptation. Ranging in seriousness from relatively harmless folk beliefs in demons that seek out women after dark, to food taboos that harm health, to the physically violent practice of female circumcision, such customs of course vary greatly in their psychological and physical effects on women.

In Sudan, Egypt, Sri Lanka, and Mexico, when I asked women in rural areas — who generally had received little if any education — whether they thought that laws should be passed to aid the advancement of women, they mostly answered "no." In contrast, the more educated women I interviewed strongly expressed the view that, without change in the legislation governing women's status within the family, no basic change in women's condition could take place. They believed that a modification in *family law* (which governs marriage rights, inheritance, polygamy, and divorce), as well as the enforcement of these rights, was essential to removing existing barriers to women's positive self-perception and to their participation and achievement in society.

In cultures where women are relegated to lower status within the family, where they have no say in the choice of their husbands, and where they have little or no decision-making authority, they frequently lack self-respect as well. This is clear in what they say as they describe

47

their lives or their feelings about personal worth. An illiterate peasant woman I talked with in Tunisia said to me: "Just look at me! I am nothing but a beast." She was an older woman who had been married at age thirteen, long before Tunisia's laws were changed to protect and aid women. I heard similar, self-deprecating remarks from many women in the other countries I visited.

On a Sri Lankan plantation, I spoke with a woman who had gone to school for three years—just long enough to learn to read and write. She worked and lived in relative comfort on a banana and coconut plantation that had recently become a cooperative settlement. She was forty-five years old, married, and had four children. As a worker in the coopera-tive, she was entitled to equal legal economic status to that of her husband and other male workers, including a share of the farm's profits. As we sat on the steps of the manager's office, overlooking a yard full of chickens, she explained that life was indeed better for her than it had been for her mother.

"It is better working on this estate now that it has become a coopera-tive farm. There is common ownership, and we have a right to join in the discussions on how to run the farm. We divide the profits among our-selves. Running the farm is up to *us* now, and that is a good feeling."

Yet this same woman—like others I was to speak with—remained convinced (revealing a misinterpretation of a tenet of Buddhism) that she had been born a woman because she had sinned a thousand times in a previous life.

"I would rather have been a man; to be born a woman is a sin. I am a Buddhist, and to be born a man is a privilege. Those who have done good things—or have not done bad things—will have an opportunity to be born men. If men's and women's education is equal, there are no differences, really—I know that whatever a man can do, a woman can do also—but it is still a privilege to be born a man."

Her words recalled answers to the question I had asked in all six countries: "Was there ever a time when you wished you had been born a man?" The less-educated women often said "yes." With surprising fre-quency, they added comments such as, "My father would look at me and say, 'Why couldn't you have been a boy?,' " or "I feel guilty about being a girl," or "Men look down upon us—they think we are not as capable."

Neither the Sri Lankan plantation worker nor other women who said such things seemed to grasp the apparent contradictions in their statements, perhaps because they did not necessarily perceive *all* women —but only those like themselves, with no education—to be inferior to men. When I asked, for example, "If men and women received the same education, do you believe they would be equally capable?," the answers were overwhelmingly affirmative: "Yes, women are equal to men"; "Boys and girls—if they have the same chances—are the same"; or "Yes, I think women can be even better than men."

Kumari Jayawardene — the Sri Lankan political scientist and author whose views on other issues have been related previously—told me that in her talks to both rural and urban women, she tries to counsel women to not inculcate fears and superstitions in their daughters. She urges women to not discriminate against girls in their treatment of their children and to give girls the same opportunities as boys. As we talked about the problem of women's feelings of inferiority, Dr. Jayawardene expressed her concern that superstition and religion are commonly, though not overtly, *used* by men to continue to dominate and control women's lives.

"What I find—and I am referring only to informal discussions—is that men consciously use superstition and religion to keep women down. Men do not believe these things themselves. For example, take a very sophisticated man — a bureaucrat, government servant, doctor, or lawyer—who does not believe in religion. If you mention religion, he will say, 'I am not a believer.' Yet he drives his wife by car to church or to a temple and waits outside while she goes and shows all this sentiment. *He* is a superior being, you know. But his wife does all this. I questioned one such man: 'How can you, a rationalist and an atheist, possibly take your wife to a temple where she gets on all fours and prostrates herself?' He answered, 'I'm a tolerant man. When I met her she believed all this. I'm not going to force my reasoning on her.' But I began to realize that this, too, was rubbish. For her, this going out of the house is, literally, an opiate. It is her only opiate. Going out anywhere is really a big 'outing' for any woman in a situation like that—especially going out to a temple with incense and flowers and the whole atmosphere, and where she's promised grace. And the man, not believing himself, encourages it. I think this goes right through our society—that men *encourage* superstition. And women perpetuate it among their children.

"Many of the superstitions prevalent in Sri Lanka are linked to chastity. The notion of not going out after six o'clock, for example, has its basis in the protection of chastity. Women believe that there are certain devils who seek to possess women. If you walk along the street after six, the saying goes, you'll meet the 'black prince'—who is one such devil—and he will possess you. Of course, if you are accompanied by a male child, even if he's only three years old, the 'black prince' won't come anywhere near you. Or if you're carrying a male infant in your arms, you can go anywhere you like. Another belief is that women must not eat fried food when they are about to go out because, again, some evil spirit may possess them. This is a very common belief—even among young women in the large towns."

Food taboos that apply only to women are still widely observed in some of the countries I visited. Like the belief in staying home after six o'clock, these taboos often are overtly protective of women — teaching that eating a certain type of food will have some bad effect on women, but not on men. Apart from their often serious nutritional effects on women, such taboos are also likely to have psychological effects. They may well be just another way of keeping women from getting a fair share. But if girls are led to believe that they have weaknesses to this or that food, they are, after all, likely to believe that in this way, too, they are inferior to boys.

In northwestern Kenya, near the Ugandan border, I met with a group of peasant women who had gathered for a lesson in farming. We were sitting in a primary school classroom after the close of the school day. Nine women, all married and mothers, had agreed to talk to me. Among the things we discussed were the superstitions of the area, which, they said, dealt mainly with food. One neatly dressed and turbaned woman in her forties told me about a superstition that was far more prevalent when she was a little girl than it is today:

"Females were not supposed to eat chicken; only men were allowed to eat it. I don't know why. If you were found eating chicken you would be laughed at and ridiculed. The times are changing now. Although my mother doesn't eat chicken, most of us now do. We even eat eggs. Before, you weren't supposed to eat them, either. Women also are not supposed to take milk and some types of fish. And the men look for the best pieces of meat in the chicken—the gizzard and the back. We can only eat that when the husband is not there. If the husband is home, the best pieces are for him."

When we took leave of the group later in the afternoon, the interpreter explained that the common belief is that young girls should not eat chicken, because if they do, they will never find a husband. And married women should not eat chicken either; if they do, the children they bear may be deformed. "Men are not subject to these beliefs, of course," she said. "They will find a wife regardless of their diet and will not be held responsible if their children are born imperfect." Superstitious practices such as these tend to linger on even after they are no longer openly believed—since people do not feel sure that there is no basis for them.

In El Medani, Sudan, a group of educated women were willing to talk with me one afternoon about a custom of another order altogether: the circumcision of young girls. We had spent the morning traveling with the Sudanese Minister of Social Welfare, Dr. Fatma Abdul Mahmoud, listening to her speeches at gatherings in villages along the route to the dusty capital of Gezira Province. Two of the women in the group were in their early twenties. They were members of elite families of Khartoum, high school graduates, and employees of a government ministry. Both were to be married within a few months. A third woman, also in her twenties, was a law student who was preparing for her imminent wedding. The fourth woman making up our group of five was older, married, and the mother of seven children. She was from El Medani and was a volunteer in the Sudanese Women's Union there. She, too, had completed her secondary education.

Hoping to escape the mid-day heat, we had taken refuge in a rest house that had been placed at the disposal of the minister. During our conversation, one woman brought up the subject of female circumcision, and one by one, each woman present wanted to talk about it at length.

The views these women expressed seemed somewhat ambivalent. Although they all voiced liberal "theories" on women's rights — and behavior — they nevertheless showed a surprising willingness to perpetuate in practice the very customs they condemned. They said that virginity should not be considered important — even arguing that it would be better to have relations with a man before marriage, in order to know him well. Moreover, although they said they believed the practice of circumcision to be harmful and useless, when I asked if they would circumcise their daughters, they all said, "Yes, I will have to." Clearly these women did not yet dare to act according to their expressed convictions — a reflection of how entrenched the custom of circumcision, particularly, remains in their part of the world.

We talked for a long time about marriage customs and about virginity and the issue of premarital relations. All four of the women agreed with the views expressed by one of them — the twenty-three-year-old government employee — on the question of sexual relations before marriage:

"It is normal. Youth believes it is normal, but out of respect for the family we cannot do it. I am going to marry in January. I know the man I will marry. I know him and I see him often. But if my family knew that I was even just seeing him, they would not accept it. Lots of couples get to know each other only on the telephone. They talk for hours on the phone, but they have only seen each other once at a wedding or some other family event.

"Yet in some tribes in Sudan, there are practices that are forbidden to us. In the south and in some places in the western provinces, if the girl doesn't get acquainted with the man and have a baby, he doesn't marry her. In the southern part of Sudan, they used to insist on pregnancy before marriage."

When I asked this same young woman what she personally thought about this issue, she replied:

"I think it is normal. Otherwise, you see, there is the problem of prostitution. That is the outcome of not allowing girls to get acquainted with boys. I think we should be allowed to get to know each other."

The other women nodded in agreement and themselves brought up discussion of other sex problems as we continued our conversation. One pointed out that custom dictates that women must feign indifference to sexual pleasure:

"Sudanese women are not allowed to show any pleasure in making love. That is the reason for the clitorectomy—so that we don't have any desire. But if it were to happen that you felt something, you couldn't say anything, since that would mean you had had a previous experience — that you were a bad woman. So even if you do feel something, you just keep quiet."

As we talked, each woman wanted to relate the story of her own circumcision, each describing the process in more detail than the last.

51

One, a twenty-five-year-old social worker, had experienced the most radical form of the practice — the pharaonic circumcision, which involves excising the clitoris and cutting off a portion of both sides of the labia minora and majora. The flesh is then sewn together, leaving only a small opening for the menses and urine. The young woman described how it had been done:

"I was just eight years old. There is always a special woman — the midwife — who does it in her house. It takes five people to hold you. All your neighbors and family come. They want to watch. It is like a tribal ceremony. One gets presents and money, just like a bride. My grandmother took me and had the operation done. They took me off to the Nile at sunset. Sometimes it is difficult to find a stream. You have to wash for three or four days, and you can't urinate because it burns too much. Before medicine came to Sudan, they would cut the girl and tie up her legs with a rope for forty days until she healed.

"I will have to do it to my daughters. My mother has her opinion, and all the family have their say. My grandmother, for example, would ask me, 'Why don't you want to do it?' And she would be very angry; she would think that my daughter will be in more danger if this is not done. It is almost compulsory here."

The young woman hesitated a moment, seemingly waiting for me to react. I asked, "What happens when you marry and have relations — if you are sewn up like that?"

"The opening is so small it takes a long time for the man to penetrate — sometimes one month, sometimes two weeks. The man enjoys it being tight, and after one or two years he will help you go and rearrange yourself — to have the operation that makes you tight again."

This "tightening" operation apparently is not uncommon. The married woman of the group confirmed that her husband had asked her to go and have herself resewn, "tightened up." She seemed to accept his request as normal. She had had seven children and thus had been sewn together eight times. Now she would undergo a ninth stitching for what she believes to be her husband's right to pleasure.

Dr. Osman Madawi, the chief gynecologist at the hospital in Khartoum, is one of a group of Sudanese doctors who are trying to educate the public on the dangers of circumcision. He explained to me some of the secondary effects of the practice:

"The main problem is hemorrhage, the second is infection (urinary tract, tetanus), and then there is also the damage done to other parts of the anatomy. The clitoris and the sensitive part of the labia are partly removed, and that reduces desire in a woman. But the amount of reduction? I don't think it is much — but definitively there is *some* reduction in desire.

"Originally, the main reason for the practice was to protect virginity, the other reason being the reduction of sensitivity. They leave an opening that is large enough for the urine to pass through but not large enough for intercourse. At childbirth, of course, we have to do a routine episiotomy on the woman before the child can be born."

I asked Dr. Madawi what psychological effects he thought circumcision has on women. His answer was not fully persuasive, though certainly impeccable in its logic:

"I don't think there would be any," he said, "since it is the normal thing to do. If you go against the norm, then there is a psychological effect. But the norm among the women is circumcision. Whenever you are within the norm, you don't get psychological repercussions."

I told Dr. Madawi about what the young women in El Medani had told me: that circumcision was done mostly to please the man. He did not agree. His own view was that "the husbands usually go along with it to please the mother and the grandmother. It's not the other way around."

These differing notions of why female circumcision continues to be practiced were one of many examples I encountered of a seeming lack of communication between men and women—even within the same family. The young women I interviewed in El Medani believed that circumcision pleases the man. Married women told me they would not tell their husbands that they are against the practice. It is possible that, as Dr. Madawi suggested, many of their husbands condone it mainly because they believe that the women in their families want the practice to be continued.

In Egypt, Nawal Es Saadawi—the medical doctor and author quoted earlier—told me of the repercussions of her own attempts to enlighten the public on customs relating to virginity and chastity in women. While her children did their homework in the next room of her Cairo apartment, Dr. Saadawi told me of her experience with authorities who felt challenged by the criticism of traditions that hinder the advancement of women. She had worked in the field of mental health and health education for many years, but lost her post in the Ministry of Health—where she had served as director of the general health education department—because of the books she wrote about the status of women in Egypt and other countries in the Arab world.

Dr. Saadawi told me that when she started writing in the late 1950s, her books were "revolutionary, more or less," but because they were fiction—both novels and short stories—"nobody made a row." It was when she started to write social and medical studies—studies in which there were statistics and direct attacks on tradition and religion and the structure of the family, on the relationship between men and women, as well as on those aspects of the political and the economic system that she perceived to create or exacerbate the problems of women—it was only then that both religious leaders and politicians began to feel that all this was dangerous and began to react.

"I was calling for political freedom, economic freedom, social freedom, mental freedom—and sexual freedom, too," Dr. Saadawi told me, "but they picked the one thing, the sensitive area of sex, and they blew it up all out of proportion.

"I had started my medical career as a physician in the country, in one of the villages, and I wrote about some of the cases I had seen — about virginity, about the circumcision of girls, about illegal pregnancies. I just wrote about some cases. It was the facts, not the fiction, that got me into trouble.

"In Egypt, you see," Dr. Saadawi explained, "virginity is very highly prized, and this creates a lot of problems for the medical profession — because we can't prove virginity. Some blood showing on the wedding night is taken to be the proof of virginity. But more than 30 per cent of girls don't show blood because of an elastic hymen. And these girls are punished while they are really innocent. In upper Egypt, they even may be killed if they are not virgins. Certainly the husbands will divorce them if they are not proven virgins. So I wrote about virginity, about the social and medical problems related to it—that it is not even a question of being 'honorable' or not. And that honor is in any case related to the mind, *not* to the hymen.

"I also spoke about female circumcision, because it is still practiced in Egypt, in Sudan, and in other countries—not only the Arab countries, but also some parts of South America. They excise the clitoris when the girl is a child so that she will keep her virginity. In the villages they say, 'We are going to circumcise her so she will not run after men.' Sometimes it is done as early as five, six, or seven.

"When giving gynecological examinations to Sudanese women, I was astonished. I found no labia majora, no labia minora, no clitoris. They were all closed up by one long suture. At marriage there is a lot of bleeding because this suture is torn. And at childbirth the woman is torn apart, with profuse bleeding and a lot of complications.

"They call it pharaonic circumcision, but it has nothing to do with the Pharaohs. Actually, in ancient Egypt, women were equal to men. In Egypt we have female goddesses and male gods. Only since Judaism did God become male only. In Judaism, in Christianity, and in Islam, God is male. All prophets are male. But before that, in ancient religion and in ancient Egypt, we also had female goddesses and queens. Women were even portrayed the same size as men in sculpture, explicitly signifying that they were equal.

"I wrote about all of these subjects from the historical and anthropological view as well. I used my medical knowledge and then read anthropology and history in order to understand how the circumcision 'operation,' for example — which is, I think, a remnant of the ancient practice of the chastity belt — had come about. Do you know why men first came to oppress women sexually? When man started to establish his patriarchal family, it was impossible for him to ascertain his fatherhood unless he forced monogamy on women. If a woman married two men, he would never know which were his children. So he forced monogamy on women. He did not do this because he loved his children and his wife, but for the economic reasons of inheritance. So man enjoys sex and polygamy and mistresses while he forces the 'chastity belt' on his wife — he circumcises her.

"But how could men enforce monogamy? After all, women are polygamous by nature from the sexual point of view. Human beings, male and female, are polygamous by nature. When men started to insist on monogamy in women, they had to enforce it by sexual and economic oppression, by legal and religious oppression. That's why the oppression of women was the most pronounced of all.

"Man oppressed woman in all respects. He isolated her in the home, he fed her, and he deprived her of paid work. And she still continues to work without payment for his children and his home. Millions of peasant women work for their husbands. They work day and night in the field and in the house with no payment. This is economic exploitation and oppression by 'chastity belt.' "

Attitudes about the importance of virginity vary to some extent among the regions and ethnic groups I visited. Thus in some rural areas of Mexico, a young woman may be "stolen" from her family by the future husband, and the elopement is condoned by others until a child or several children are born. Then it is considered better to marry officially, so that the children can be baptized.

Among some tribes of Kenya and Sudan, a young woman often is expected to "prove" that she can become pregnant before the marriage takes place. Victoria Yar Arol, the young member of the People's Regional Assembly of Southern Sudan (whose views on other points were recounted earlier), described to me some of the origins of Sudanese practices relating to virginity, and went on to tell me about the function of the bride price:

"Here in the southern part of Sudan, it is very different from the Moslem north. Far back in our history, the tribes of the south never had this concern for virginity. Now there are a few families who have imported this idea from the north, but traditionally our notion of 'virginity' was not based on whether or not a girl was found to be a virgin; it was based on what the tribe knew of the girl — whether she was being married directly from her home without first indulging in bad habits. If you were known to be a loose girl, that was one thing; but if you had lost your virginity without anybody knowing, nobody really worried about it — provided that you were officially married and a bride price was paid.

"In the Dinka tribe, for example, the relatives of the man go to the relatives of the girl and propose marriage. The people sit together and agree on a bride price. Once they have agreed on the number of cows to be given as the dowry, the relatives of the future husband return home to their village. They prepare the number of cows agreed upon and then invite the elders of the girl's family to come to inspect the cows. If they are satisfied with the quality and quantity of the cows, the marriage is accepted.

"Recently there have been questions about the bride price being undesirable. People say that it reduces the woman's dignity, as if she were not human and could be looked upon as mere property. But when you consider it carefully, you find that in the traditional homes divorce is very rare, because the bride price is not only a *personal* transaction. When a bride price is paid and a girl is married, she is considered the property of her husband's whole family. Our families here are very large. Likewise, when the girl's family receives the bride price from the bridegroom's family, it is distributed to the different members of the girl's family and often is used to obtain wives for her brothers. So when a divorce takes place, it does not necessarily end with the divorce of that one couple; it can cause other divorces as well. For example, if the bride's brother's wife was 'bought' with her bride price, the brother may first have to divorce his own wife in order to get back the cattle that must be returned to his sister's husband."

I interrupted Victoria Yar Arol to ask whether the bride price can therefore be looked upon as a protective measure for the wife. She said that this could indeed be so—provided that the wife was considered a worthy member of the clan by other members of her husband's family—because then:

"If the husband is not nice to her, his relatives are likely to come and talk to him and to tell him that he should treat her more pleasantly. The whole clan's welfare may be involved in *her* welfare."

Some other important economic ramifications of the bride price custom were explained to me by a group of illiterate peasant women in a Kenyan village. I questioned this group of older women about the bride price practices in their own families. We were sitting in a circle, and each woman around the circle in turn told me that she had been "bought" with "four cows and a goat," or "two cows and five goats"—each showing a certain pride in mentioning her "price." One older woman then turned to me, asking, "When you were married, how much did your husband pay to your family?"

I explained that in the United States there was rarely a specific "bride price" involved in marriages. My explanation first brought a burst of laughter from the group, but almost immediately I noticed very puzzled expressions on the faces of several women.

"But if your husband didn't pay any bride price for you," they asked with great seriousness, "how are you going to help your parents when they are old? When your father dies and leaves your mother, how is she going to live without your bride price?"

Whether the bride price is considered a payment to the parents of the girl for having raised her well, or whether it serves as a part of the parents' old-age security, the financial transactions involved in exchanging brides and bridegrooms result in designating a woman's "value." In Sri Lanka, for example, it is the bride's family that offers a dowry to the husband. But as Dr. Jayawardene pointed out, dowry practices are changing:

"In certain parts of Sri Lanka, the dowry is traditional: the daughter has to be given a certain amount of money or land at the time of her marriage as an offering to her husband. In other parts of Sri Lanka, the practice has changed. A dowry of land and goods was a feudal institution. Now, with capitalism, the dowry has taken on a capitalistic form. You can measure a girl's worth by her job. A job bringing $500 a year— if you calculate that for twenty years—represents quite a sum of money. It becomes like a dowry. Thus you don't necessarily search for a family with a lump sum, but for one with a girl who has a job.

"This is not so throughout Sri Lanka, however. In areas like Jaffna, in the north of the island—where there is a large Hindu population— the dowry is a great problem for anyone with daughters. There the dowry has to be a lump sum of cash; they don't care about the job. Resolving that problem has become a fine art. For example, you can look for a family with both a son and a daughter and try to arrange for your daughter to marry their son, and for your son to marry their daughter. That way there is no dowry exchange, only a son-daughter exchange."

In Kankesanturai, in the north of Sri Lanka, I met a social worker who had been saving for her daughter's dowry since the day the child was born. "I want to be able to get a good husband for her," she said, "and to do that I must save much money. If I don't, she will not be able to find an educated husband."

Malsiré Dias, a professor of sociology at the University of Colombo, explained how the dowry system has evolved along with the changing economic system in Sri Lanka:

"Traditionally, the dowry was really a *gift* — given to the daughter on leaving her ancestral home. It really belonged to her. Now it has become more of a business transaction among a certain social class. They advertise the dowry and then give the daughter in marriage to the young man who offers the most potential for the price. Before, the marriage was arranged on other grounds, and the dowry came only later — as a gift. I am opposed to this new idea of a business transaction. It demeans the woman."

Surely it might be argued that such business transactions are demeaning to the husbands as well. In fact, however, the husband is favored: he gains wealth, goods, or potential income *plus* a wife to bear his children. The wife, on the other hand, simply enters another family, where her dependent status remains substantially unchanged.

Dr. Dias smiled a moment and asked me whether I had already heard about the Sri Lankan custom of horoscope matchmaking.

"There is a belief that one must consult the horoscope when arranging a marriage. Astrology is a sort of fate written according to the time of birth, and when it comes to a marriage, you are matched. Of course it is the female who is matched against the male's horoscope. You have to get marks out of twenty characteristics. If you get eighteen out of twenty, then the marriage is perceived as a good one."

The customs enumerated in this chapter merely serve to illustrate a far greater number of practices by which women's lives in many societies (including the six countries I visited) continue to be far more controlled than those of men. Some of these practices clearly have destructive psychological and even physical effects on women. Most are demeaning to women as full-fledged human beings and act as barriers to their self-image—and therefore to the realization of their personal potential.

Since these practices are based on beliefs held by many people, including women, they are firmly entrenched and generally can be phased out only over time by a slow process of change through education, example, and leadership. As Dr. Nawal Es Saadawi emphasized, however, women are also oppressed by customs that could be more rapidly eliminated through legislation.

"In Egypt," Dr. Saadawi pointed out, "a man can divorce his wife without cause—without giving any reason. Often women actually go on having many children *because* of the divorce system. Since it is her husband who has all the rights in a divorce, a woman may have ten or twenty children in the belief that this way she will be able to capture him. If we are to improve the status of women, we first have to change those laws whose impact on the status of women is really scandalous: the marriage and divorce laws. I would start with these first, because that would have immediate effects. Education and changing attitudes take more time. First we must change family law."

As countries which have passed such legislation have found out, however, the mere existence of laws that prohibit "blind" marriages, polygamy, whimsical divorces, and the beating of wives does not automatically remedy the injustices perpetrated. Nor does it eliminate (or even lessen) women's sense of insecurity. To become full participants in society, women must be helped to understand that they are equal before the law; and the laws must be enforced.

Early one morning I met with a group of women who had gathered to plan their participation in the agricultural show of Mombasa, Kenya. The group consisted of Christian and Moslem women who were volunteers in programs for the advancement of women in the Mombasa area.

When I asked these women about the practice of polygamy, many of them replied with obvious emotion. Each told stories of how polygamy places a burden on the lives of women and thus on the lives of other family members. One woman said:

"If you meet a man who has four wives and who are all suffering from hunger and lack of care, and if you ask that man, 'Why all this?,' he will just answer, 'It is allowed by my religion.' The salaries are low and there are many children, so there is hunger."

A second woman spoke up to point out that there is not much women can do about it—since legal action is itself in the hands of men:

"The problem of polygamy is not taken seriously in government. I think it is really up to *women* to speak out strongly against it. There should be a law: 'one man, one woman.' But you see, who is going to voice this? We have more men than women in parliament. And each man has three wives. So *they* won't agree to outlaw polygamy. There was a law once that if a man got a girl pregnant he would have to maintain the child until it reached adulthood. That law was abolished because many parliament members were such fathers themselves. So the men are really oppressing the women, and in Kenya there is nobody to force them to do otherwise."

Another common practice in the countries I visited—as elsewhere, including the developed countries—is wife beating. Countless women came up to me after the group discussions I conducted to ask me in a hushed, half-ashamed way: "What would you do if you had a husband who beat you?" In the non-Moslem areas, the question often was: "What should I do about my husband's drinking?" When I asked these women whether their husbands also beat them, they usually answered: "Yes, when he drinks." A serious problem is that wife beating is rarely prohibited by law or by religion. "Man is the master," or "Man has the authority" are some of the replies women gave to questions on why wife beating is permitted. "The priest speaks out about it," said one peasant woman in Mexico, "but the men pay no heed."

Moreover, where privacy is a luxury that only the very rich can afford, wife beating is an almost public act. Neighbors as well as the entire family know when a man is beating his wife. Yet women themselves, ashamed of their situation, frequently remain silent.

One young woman in Dolores Hidalgo, Mexico, told me of her husband's drinking and of the violence in which it usually resulted. She was twenty-four years old and was unhappy with her marriage. Her husband was a ticket collector on a bus line, and, to supplement the family budget, she had found part-time sales work in a bakery. She had not wanted to leave her baby daughter with a neighbor in order to go to work, but she said that since her husband drank away most of his earnings, she had had no choice but to go to work. When I asked this woman what the women of her town needed most, she replied:

"They need understanding husbands. On Saturdays the men get paid, so Saturday and Sunday they spend all day drinking. On Monday, none of the men in this town work. They spend their money on drinking and give very little to their wives. My own husband likes to drink. After work he always goes to the cantina, and he usually beats me when he returns drunk."

Yet women rarely rebel in any effective manner against this type of violence. For example, in a village near Le Kef, Tunisia, Zoubaida, a young girl who was not yet married and who had had the benefit of a secondary school education—spoke to me of male violence with surprising resignation. At the time we met, Zoubaida was seventeen and attending a craft class sponsored by the National Union of Tunisian Women. She had learned how to weave traditional patterned rugs and was looking forward to the day when she could buy her own loom from her earnings. She said she would like to see other women improve as she has done, perhaps even more. She said she would like to help them find work and continue their studies—to help them to go beyond her own situation.

When I asked Zoubaida, "What do you consider to be the ideal age for marriage?," she replied:.

"Twenty-five; because a girl first must learn how to take care of a home, raise children, learn how to live with a husband—all the education that makes for a good marriage. I don't know whether or not my father will let me meet my husband before the wedding, but I hope that we will get along."

Clearly Zoubaida was a well-informed and active young village woman. The thoughts she expressed about her situation showed her intelligence, awareness, and concern for the plight of women. Yet when I asked her what she would do if her husband beat her, she replied:

"I would accept it. If I was at fault and my husband beat me, I would accept it. If he accused me wrongly, I would try to convince him, to discuss it with him — I might leave for a time and go to my mother's house—but I would always come back. But if I was at fault, I would not say anything."

In Sri Lanka, as in most of the countries I visited, I was told that violence against wives is not something with which authorities concern themselves. As Dr. Kumari Jayawardene pointed out:

"It just is not an issue. It is considered legal. The husband has the *right.* In every way he is the master—superior in wisdom and intellect. So the chastisement of wives is considered normal. I don't know how often it occurs, but it is accepted."

Superstitions, taboos, and a residue of demeaning customs continue to restrict women to roles that allow for little self-esteem. If these factors are to disappear from the lives of the next generation—if the expectation is that women are to lead fuller and more useful lives in the future—the role of leadership is enormously important.

An indication of what constructive national leadership can do to upgrade women's self-esteem and enhance their contribution to both family and national life was apparent in many of my conversations with women in Tunisia. In El Giref, a village in the central part of the country, I talked with an elderly woman, the wife of a small landowner who had parlayed his small holdings into a comfortable existence. She was the mother of seven — four sons and three daughters. The sons had been educated; one was an engineer, the other a lawyer. But the daughters had remained unschooled and were married at puberty.

Sitting in the central room of her small home, this elderly woman told me about her life. When I asked her age, she said: "I don't know. I don't even know how to read or write, so how do you think I would ever know things like my age?" As she talked on, her voice became more high-pitched. Anger seemed to enter into her thoughts as she told me about her lack of education and of her illiteracy. She judged the past with great disdain and spoke of the "new ways" with approval and confidence — mentioning several times how much the President of Tunisia had done for women:

"There is a big difference between my granddaughters and me," she said. "When I was a girl, we couldn't go out of the house. We didn't meet our husbands until the wedding. We didn't know them at all. They just gave us to a man. Now women are educated, they work, and they know their husbands. That's very different.

"I had to learn many new things along the way. I had to learn hygiene, to take better care of my children, and to give them an education different from my own. We learned by imitating each other, by watching other women and how *they* did things.

"Before, women were unhappy. They were always in poor health, nursing the children, having children, always weak. Now women are flourishing. They can take advantage of all that is offered. They can have family planning and be in good health. They are clean and healthy and have freedom."

When I asked whether she talked about these things with other women, she replied:

"That's all we talk about—family planning, women's freedom. We talk about all the subjects that concern women. In my day, because we were not educated, we lived like beasts. We didn't know anything. It is obvious that we were always bypassed by men."

I asked her if she thought men were happy to see women taking advantage of these changes.

"In any case, it's none of their business," she replied. "We are equal. The President says so—it's all thanks to him. So even if the husbands are not happy about all these changes, they can't do anything about them. Now women can go to buy things by themselves; they have the choice to come and go. Their husbands can't forbid it any more. It is much better. But still there are problems for all the women of the world anyway. Not just Tunisian women. All women are reaching out to learn, to go out, to listen. Not only us. All the women of the world."

# 5

NUTRITION, HEALTH, AND FAMILY PLANNING

# "I'm just too tired
## with the work and these babies"

### NUTRITION, HEALTH, AND FAMILY PLANNING

The town of Busia, near the Ugandan border of Kenya, is fortunate to have a fine, modern hospital. There, a young midwife who had returned to the region after obtaining her training in Nairobi talked with me about some of the health problems in the area. Discussing malnutrition and health in general, she observed that in most poor areas, nutritional problems arise "because there is a large family" or because "there just isn't enough food produced on the family plot or enough money to feed so many people." The situation in her own region, however, was due to another problem — one that also contributes to malnutrition in many other parts of the world:

"The poor health here is not a poverty problem. There is plenty of land. The problem is the lack of knowledge about nutrition. That's one thing that has to be learned. If people knew how to utilize foods and what to plant to feed the children, it would be better. For example, here they plant groundnuts. They take these nutritious groundnuts to markets and sell them in order to obtain needed cash; then they buy bread, for example, from which they get less nutritional value. It doesn't make any sense. What we need here is health-nutrition education.

"Before, we had many nutritional field workers, but now our clinic is training those field workers to be nurses as well. They will be going out to teach both health and nutrition in the villages.

"We also have malaria here. In fact, most of our patients — adults and children — first come in to our clinic for malaria treatment. For the eight months I have served here, I have been encouraging mothers to come in not only for that, but also to bring their children to our health-care class. Nutritional problems contribute to the mortality rate. Many children die from just measles. A child who suffers from measles and has not been well fed just wears down completely.

"The nutritional problem is also due to some of the superstitions and taboos. There are still many areas where people believe children should not eat eggs because, they say, the children will never talk. You just have to keep persuading people. When mothers realize that children who eat eggs *do* talk, they will convince other mothers that their children will not be harmed by eggs. But you can't *force* them to suddenly change what they do. First I ask them to try other things that give the same food nutrients as eggs. Women are not supposed to eat chicken either — although the men do. It's not fair."

The interrelated health problems this young midwife described are not unique to this area—or to Kenya. The vicious circle of nutrition and infection persists in most developing countries. Over the past twenty years, many of these nations have undertaken ambitious programs to provide health-care services for their citizens and have built remarkable health-care systems upon the nucleus of medical facilities left by the European colonial powers. In many cases, an attempt has been made to provide health services to both the rural and urban populations.

The costs of improving what in most places still remains an inadequate and sometimes ill-designed medical infrastructure have been enormous — especially for countries whose national economies are neither prosperous nor stable. Most developing nations had but a handful of trained medical personnel when they became independent. Where there were no medical schools, young people were urged and helped to study abroad; where trained medical or paramedical personnel was scarce, efforts were made to find foreigners with these skills through development assistance programs from the U.N. World Health Organization and other international agencies.

Yet in many developing countries, medical centers and hospitals are still scarce, poorly situated for serving the greatest possible number of people, and often both insufficiently and inappropriately staffed and equipped. It is impractical and costly to equip remote areas with infirmaries and medical personnel. In existing facilities, medical officers are often overworked and underpaid, resulting in some cases in corrupt medical administrations. Even in the most fortunate of developing countries, the provision of adequate health services will necessitate continuing investments and medical training programs for many years to come.

It should be stated, however, that the positive impact of decades of improvements in health services has been vast. As health care reached out to rural areas, infant mortality rates decreased dramatically; increasing numbers of the sick and injured survived. As a result, however, the population growth rate has increased rapidly, creating an even greater demand for health services: more immunization programs, medical facilities, and clean water sources. But, despite the efforts made to provide health care, the lives of many rural people throughout the developing world continue to be plagued by a variety of diseases and afflictions, ranging from elephantiasis, malaria, tuberculosis, and gastroenteritis to hookworms and taenia — and many of these afflictions necessitate vast public health campaigns on a scale too costly for individual nations.

In many developing nations, including some of those I visited, the high incidence of malnutrition continues to be the primary health problem. Inadequate nutrition and hunger weaken an individual's resistance to disease at any age. And, in the poorer areas of the world, malnutrition — resulting in acute anemia — is especially widespread among women and children.

Many of the officials with whom I spoke, including the young Kenyan midwife, emphasized that malnutrition results not only from poverty, but from ignorance about nutritional needs as well. Throughout the world, the preparation (as well as cultivation, preservation, storage, and apportioning) of the family's food supply has traditionally been the responsibility of women. But the variety of foods available to women in poorer regions generally is limited—not only because of lack of cash or land, but also because of local cultivation practices and the absence of effective food marketing systems. Moreover, the cultivation of cash crops has disrupted traditional diets, which quite often were fairly nutritious. A major factor in this equation seems to be that few women have knowledge of the nutritional value of foods that are available in these changing circumstances. Without such knowledge, they do not know how to supplement local staples with foods that could be grown on family plots; and they tend to buy the least expensive foods—which often have less nutritive value.

Medical officers in the plantation area around Maskeliya, Sri Lanka, told me that anemia is very common among the region's women—because of the combination of poor nutrition, the burden of childbearing, and the heavy labor that the women perform. In this mountainous region of central Sri Lanka, women are employed on large tea plantations as pluckers. They work long hours on the steep hillsides, plucking the ripe tea leaves from shoulder-high bushes. At day's end, they carry the harvest to a factory in eighty-pound baskets that have remained strapped to their backs throughout the day. It is grueling work, and the wages are low: some 4.70 rupees (U.S. $.45) per day.

While the tea plucking is done by the women, the men are employed at other hard-labor tasks — breaking ground for new tea bushes to be planted, or digging up the worn out plants. The plantation workers live in a series of long bungalows built along the steep hillsides. Each bungalow is subdivided into separate quarters for four families. There is no water or electricity in the one room and kitchen allotted to each family.

I had a chance to talk with one of the tea pluckers at the end of her workday. She insisted that I wait while she changed from her work sari into a better one — a worn mauve sari that she reserved for special occasions. She was a thin woman and appeared devoid of energy as we sat talking on the doorstep of her bungalow. Thirty-five years old and illiterate, she had worked in the fields since the age of ten. She told me she had not seen much improvement in her life. For years, she had coped with the problems of caring for a large family, poor hygiene, and a decreasing income (due to inflation).

"I had nine children, but I lost the ninth just a year ago. The eighth child is three years old. I have five sons and three daughters. I never went to school. I was just twelve when I was married. I had not seen my husband before. My marriage was arranged by my parents. I had my first child at the age of thirteen.

"When I was a small child, I was quite all right, since my mother had only three children. But now I find life extremely difficult because I have such a large family. That's the main reason. If people have more than three children, they find it difficult to manage."

When I asked her what she thought would ease the life of the women tea pluckers on the estate, she replied:

"Many have very large families, and we are lodged in these bungalow rooms. There is hardly any space. There are too many people, and one room is not enough for a large family. We now have to ask the superintendent for another room, and it will be more expensive for us. If we weren't so many, the problem wouldn't arise.

"The other problem is hygiene. We do have tap water, but it should be improved. There is only one faucet—300 yards away—for more than twenty families. We should have a better water supply and toilets. That is what we need, water and lavatories."

This tea plucker's life is difficult, of course, but compared to the lives of women in rural areas throughout the developing world, her situation is relatively secure. She does have a constant source of income, even if it is meager. She lives in a permanent building and has access to a nearby source of tap water. For many of the women with whom I spoke in still poorer regions, these advantages were nonexistent. The strength of most rural women is continually drained by working in the fields, walking miles a day in search of water or firewood, cooking, pregnancies, and caring for children. And, knowing that their children do not have enough to eat, mothers in the world's poorer nations often nurse their infants for two, three, and even four years. Both mother and child are weakened as a result.

In Sudan, I spoke with Dr. Aziz Malik, chief gynecologist of the Port Sudan city hospital. He singled out anemia as a major health problem of women in that region.

"In about 80 per cent of our cases, the hemoglobin level is far below normal. This is attributed to nutritional inadequacies. That is why we get such a high incidence of spontaneous abortion. Premature births are high, and this, too, is mainly due to inadequate nutrition. Here in the hospital, we get about four cases of miscarriage per day—all from poor nutrition. The people here eat just milk and meat—milk from the goats and cattle meat. They have absolutely no concept of eating vegetables, or of how to cook them. The vegetables come from very far away, so they are expensive. But even that isn't the real reason. The problem is that people don't know what makes for a proper diet."

I later visited a family of nomadic origin that lived a mile or two from Port Sudan. They were members of the camel-owning Beja tribe of the Red Sea hills. Several years before, the family had come to the outskirts of Port Sudan, where it settled in a wooden shack-like structure. The husband then left to find work in another town along the coast. He returns every six months or so with the money he has been able to save.

His wife — a small-boned, delicate, and extremely thin woman — said she thought she was about thirty years old. She kept a frayed veil draped over half of her face, and had I not been told her age, I would have guessed from her demeanor and appearance that she was at least fifteen years older. She told me that eighteen family members are crowded into their quarters and share the meager portions of food available. Two of the woman's children died at birth, but two are still living. One of them, a boy about three years old, was running around the courtyard naked as we talked. The woman said she didn't know why her children had died but that she had had a "fever just before childbirth, and the children were born dead."

I asked if there had been any other health problems in the family.

"No . . . no disease. We are just tired all the time. We grind beans to make flour, then cook the flour with water. It makes a sort of porridge. We serve it with milk. We have butter from goat's milk and a few dates. That's all. It's like that every day."

Although this food mix was a relatively nutritious one, the quantity available was insufficient to feed the large family. My host did, however, have one appreciable resource: a public source of clean water. The public tap was a few feet from her door.

Another member of the Beja tribe, a woman I visited in a desert setting forty miles south of Port Sudan, was not as lucky. Her surroundings were sand, flies, and desert winds. Her home consisted of a few sticks stuck into the sand to which palm leaves were attached, providing a degree of privacy and a constant draft so treasured in the desert heat. The dirt floor was covered with a straw mat, and a few utensils were piled in one corner.

When I asked the woman what she thought women of the area needed most, she replied:

"A clinic for health. We should have a trained midwife and a water supply. We have to walk about a mile to get our water, and the water is not good. It is too salty. We have to distill it ourselves and it takes much time."

I asked how far it was to the nearest doctor.

"Port Sudan, forty miles to the north. My family is rarely sick—but I am—I am always tired."

Widowed several years before, left without income and with only a few possessions, this woman had settled her family of three children near a one-room wooden schoolhouse, attended by the children of nomads when their families are not traveling. The woman's only earnings were those she received from time to time in payment for cleaning the school. When she offered me a drink from a tin can filled with water, she said, "I don't have anything else to offer you. We are too poor."

The need for a qualified midwife expressed by this Sudanese woman was one I heard repeatedly in different settings and in other countries. The midwife is, and always has been, a key figure in the lives of rural women. She is part doctor, part counselor—in some places still part sorceress—and, mostly, a confidence-inspiring person at the time of childbirth. "Western" notions of public health services often overlook the vital role of the traditional midwife in rural societies. If these women were brought into the "modern" health-care system in large numbers, by simple training programs, a powerful resource would be recruited for the improvement of public health services.

In addition to performing their tasks of childbirth assistance, midwives could also teach nutrition, hygiene, and child care as part of a cost-effective effort to deliver simple health services. As was already emphasized, most developing countries cannot at this time afford to provide sophisticated public health services to all citizens. However, elementary public health campaigns and the training of "barefoot" doctors, midwives, or nutrition and hygiene teachers could contribute rapidly to the improved health of rural families.

Several years ago, in a Saharan oasis, I witnessed a scene I will never forget. A group of children ranging in ages from two to five or six were walking together holding hands. Their eyes were encrusted with secretion and flies. Each led another in a collective attempt to find their way in blindness. The scene is not uncommon; nor is blindness from trachoma or other diseases. But such suffering could be avoided at little cost: one person trained in hygiene—working with mothers of that oasis—might have prevented the children's blindness.

The importance of training women health officers or paramedics was repeatedly emphasized by officials with whom I spoke. Women in many cultures are reluctant to be treated by male medical personnel. In Mexico, Dr. Hernandez, director of the small hospital in Dolores Hidalgo, talked about this problem, one which is common to the six countries I visited:

"The question of women going to a male doctor is a cultural problem. From childbirth on, a woman is accustomed to being treated by a midwife. If getting help means she is going to be in the care of a man, she will not want the help. A man would see her body and strange things inside her." Hesitating for a moment, Dr. Hernandez added: "It is a problem for me, as a man, to treat women patients here."

Many of the women I spoke with in Mexico and other countries confirmed the words of this physician. Cherifa Mehrez, an active volunteer in community development and family planning in Egypt, explained:

"In the villages, women will not let men doctors examine them. A woman simply won't go to the doctor; her husband won't allow it. With urban women, it is much less of a concern."

When I asked Dr. Hernandez to tell me about the health situation in Dolores Hidalgo, he added:

"The major problems are malnutrition and infectious diseases. Both are derived from poverty. Ninety-five per cent of the population here has nutritional deficiencies. Anemia in women is extremely high. I don't really understand how they keep going."

During an early morning visit to a health clinic in Vihiga, Kenya, I again talked with a male doctor (women doctors were virtually impossible to find), who confirmed that the local health problems in that region were similar to those I had witnessed elsewhere.

"We have tetanus, measles, and — in the young ones — whooping cough. They also may have worms; when the children start growing,

70

they crawl around and eat some sand and get worms. These are the things we deal with daily. We show women how to treat the children, and we encourage them to attend a health clinic. There is not too much anemia here, however. And kwashiorkor [acute protein deficiency] is not prevalent because some mothers understand what it is; they understand what they must feed their children to prevent it.

"This area is densely populated, and most of the women give birth at home; they know that if they come here we may not have a bed for them. At home, they are attended by local midwives — self-made midwives. They don't use sterile instruments. Sometimes the child is delivered outside, under a banana tree. There is not proper care—no cleanliness. That's why we get all this tetanus.

"We also have problems with the young wives. When they get married, they do not understand where to go for health care. They are ignorant of that. Then when they get pregnant, they do not know that we have what we call 'antenatal clinics.' It follows that when they have children, those children may not receive sufficient care. They may not come for vaccinations that prevent disease."

I asked the doctor what he considered to be the major needs for improved health care in that area of Kenya.

"We should have more field educators. Then, I feel, we could serve rural women. Another problem is transportation. We need vehicles and money for gasoline. But first of all, we need field workers."

In Juba, in southern Sudan, I also made a visit to the local hospital. Built during the colonial period, it was a rambling establishment consisting of several small buildings—one for each of the major health services. In the children's ward, each of the twelve beds was occupied by a tiny child watched closely by an anxious mother.

A young doctor who had only recently completed his studies abroad and returned to Sudan took me through the hospital on his rounds. He said, "Probably all the people in and around Juba have chronic malaria." He explained that the condition of the children brought to the hospital was often serious. Mothers do not seek help until the sickness is well advanced and the children alarmingly weak. Most of the children I saw were suffering from malnutrition or the results of unclean water—from kwashiorkor, diarrhea, gastroenteritis. Nearly all of them also had malaria. Wizened and white-haired from the dreaded kwashiorkor, the children were weak and passive; they barely noticed our presence as we passed by.

The young doctor believed that the major scourge of southern Sudan is malaria, and that hospitals or health clinics in the region would have no real effect on the general health of the population until malaria had been brought under control:

"Instead of spending money on physical facilities, we should concentrate on taking the classic steps to control malaria. But I don't think Sudan can afford that now. I think that those responsible for a country like ours should concentrate on major diseases that are *preventable*, rather than on, for example, the construction of a series of hospitals.

Hospitals would be a waste of money because they would focus on *curative* medicine, which really does not go to the root of the problem. We should undertake programs to train people to direct regional control programs for the various diseases, especially malaria. Tuberculosis among the cattle-owning tribes is another example of a disease that could be controlled by such cadres.

"For the moment, we don't have either the human or the material resources to do these things. Yet I find it rather difficult to accept that we have to wait until we do get the resources before trying to do something with the little we do have. We should at least be able to enlighten our people as to the real cause of their misery. Most of them still think malaria is God-sent. They don't know what it is. They also don't know that it is a fever that causes gastroenteritis. They think perhaps some devil has been sent into the stomachs of their children. Health education is important—and it needs to reach out to the villages."

The doctor's exasperation was understandable: He continues to help those who come to him, and to nurse them back to health—only to see them return suffering from the same symptoms in a few months. "Preventive public health programs *first*," he said. Curative medicine for the few is a luxury in regions of the world where debilitating diseases are still prevalent and are not yet the object of control campaigns.

In a clearing in northwestern Kenya, I met with members of the women's group of M'Bale. Their self-help cooperative has been organized by a remarkable Kenyan woman who introduced herself as Miss Janet. Crippled by a childhood case of polio, she struggled to move about the compound on her knees, to which she strapped thick leather pads. When foreign church personnel left the mission cooperative some years before, Miss Janet became the cooperative's volunteer program director. The group she directs receives foodstuffs from a foreign religious organization. Miss Janet proudly told me that, since she started the feeding program, there have been no cases of malnutrition.

"We started with a missionary from England in 1966. Up to 1970, he taught the mothers about nutrition, and he tried to teach sewing also. We don't have a sewing machine. We just use a needle. Now the missionary has gone, so we are alone and we are trying to do the job. But we don't know if we can manage it. We are trying our best, but we don't know whether we are doing well or not."

Miss Janet explained that a medical field worker visits the village twice a week and that on Monday, Wednesday, and Friday, foodstuffs are distributed to the mothers of children under five years of age.

"The food comes from a missionary group in America. The mothers pay 3 shillings [U.S. $.42] per child, and with that money we pay for the transportation of the food from the coast. We give them five pounds in all—some wheat, some cereals, some cornmeal. We mix this together and teach them how to cook it. The mothers learn how to sew and cook at the same time. We teach them many things when they come here. They all want to learn how to sew and how to use a sewing machine —if only one were available. They want to make their own dresses and their husbands' shirts and to be able to mend everything. They would be happy if we could teach them those things.

"Now we are also trying to find money so we can pay someone to plough for us so that we can plant maize. If we succeed, we will teach the women — by demonstration — how to better care for their vegetable gardens. We must teach them these simple things. They want to learn more about agriculture and how to sew."

I asked Miss Janet to question the women about their children. How many did each have?

"This woman says she has two; three died in infancy. This woman has three alive, three dead. This woman: three died, five are alive. This woman: two alive, three dead. And this other woman: one died, one is alive. Children here often die from measles. This woman says her children were stillborn. And this young woman's baby stayed in her womb for ten months; it was dead. One child died of malaria when he was one and a half, and another died at age six. We have medicine for malaria, but we send the children to the health center for innoculations first. We also give medicine through a health assistant who visits us from time to time."

I asked Miss Janet to question the women about how large a family they considered to be ideal these days—given the expense of school fees, food, and other necessities.

"Some feel they can't answer that because they think perhaps this child or that will die. Some say, 'If some die, I will have at least a few remaining.' This mother, for example, thinks that four children is a good number to look after, educate, and feed. That woman thinks that if you have three children, if God helps, you'll be able to feed them. That one says four is a good number; she could look after them and educate them. She only has two, but she says that when she has four, she will join family planning."

Although some of the rural women I met — like some within the M'Bale group — were still afraid that their children might not survive, few women with whom I spoke in the six countries thought it wise to have more than three or four children. Indeed, many realized that "children don't die as much anymore," although surprisingly few expressed an awareness that this was due to the improvement of health care in the past decades. They were aware, however, that frequent pregnancies impaired their health and made it more difficult for them to care for their families and to work both within and outside the household.

Surprisingly, many of the women I spoke with actually blamed their poverty on the fact that they had large families, commenting that this makes it more difficult to make ends meet. No matter how impoverished or uneducated they were, most women explicitly stated their desire to provide a better life for their children than they had experienced themselves. Instead of having many children — "all ignorant like myself" — they wanted fewer children whom they could provide with food, education, clothing, and a good life.

A twenty-eight-year-old Tunisian, the mother of seven children, told me she regretted having had such a large family. "It is always better to have fewer children," she said, "because then you can dress them better, feed them better, and educate them properly. I would not have had seven children if I had known about family planning before."

In Wennappuwa village in Sri Lanka, a twenty-five-year-old woman I met shared this opinion, although her situation was quite different from that of the young Tunisian. She was engaged to be married and explained that since her future husband does not have a steady income, they "will not have more than three or four children because then the children would suffer. Without property, without anything to back us up, we should have only a few children and give them the attention and love they need."

In many of my conversations with families in the six countries, lack of land was mentioned as the reason why it was difficult to provide for as many children as in the past. When I talked with a group of women working in the fields in northwestern Kenya, a thirty-five-year-old woman told me:

"It is difficult to have many children these days. Before, there was plenty of land. Families that had many children could simply dig and farm as far as they needed; but now, if you have seven sons, how will you divide up the land?"

In urban settings, too, "quality versus quantity" reasoning was frequently mentioned in relation to family size. Zahia Marzouk of the Alexandria Family Planning Association told me:

"We try to teach that a mother should not have so many children because then she can have half a loaf of bread instead of a quarter of a loaf, and because she can have two dresses instead of one. She can go out to the movies if she wants to — since the family will have twice as much money. If they don't have extra money, she will not go anywhere."

In Cairo, Ingi Rouchdy, a journalist, also told me that "most women who work are planning their families because of the lack of housing, lack of services, lack of kindergartens, and lack of nurseries. They are *obliged* to limit their children to one or two." She was emphatic in expressing her opinion about one of the problems that women encounter when they wish to limit the number of children they bear:

"Somebody should convince the men as well as the women, because a child is made by the two. In Egypt, the man, with all the power he has — economic, divorce, polygamy, and all that — is still supreme. Traditionally, even women say that 'he is the master.' "

❧

Indeed, I found that although many of the women I interviewed wanted to limit the number of their pregnancies, for both economic and health reasons, they said that they were not free to make the decision on their own. They acknowledged that their anxiety about being thought infertile (and thus worthless as women), as well as their fear of the reactions of their husbands or other family members, held them back from taking advantage of family planning services — where such services were in fact available.

The idea of daring to ask their husbands if they would permit the use of a contraceptive seemed impossible, frightening — or, at least, extremely difficult — to many of the women I interviewed. Some said: "If I don't give him a child every year, he will go and get another wife. Then what will the children and I do?" Others told me: "Such matters are not discussed among men and women." Many said: "I don't want to have all these children, but my husband wants more sons," or, "I am tired. Look at me. I am nothing but a beast working in the fields and bearing all these children. I don't want any more children, but my husband says I must have as many as come."

Yet we know that women have traditionally resorted to a myriad ways to prevent or end unwanted pregnancies. Some of these methods are without serious side effects. Others (like prolonged breast-feeding) may aggravate malnutrition in both mothers and children, or (like many home-induced abortions) may result in damage to the mother's health. Still others, based on mistaken beliefs and superstitions, are totally ineffective.

In Mexico, officials at the National Population Council estimate that over one million "homemade" abortions are performed each year. Indeed, abortion and homemade contraceptives are prevalent in many cultures. I was told tales about talismans, abortive teas, charmed coconuts, and homemade pills. Some women said they had even swallowed mothballs in the hope of terminating another pregnancy. In Tunisia, a rural woman I met laughed as she said:

"When I think of all the things I ate or swallowed, hoping that they would prevent me from having another child! But they didn't work. Now it is better because I have an IUD [intrauterine device].

"Before, we made potions from castor oil leaves and other plants. Some women used magic, like the baby's dried umbilical cord. When it has fallen from the child, you soak it in water and then stuff it with a very bitter powder. I don't know the name, but it's very bitter to taste. And then you hang the cord either on the mother's ear or around her neck. That way women think they will not get pregnant again. It is a custom. It is like magic."

False rumors about modern contraceptive methods are often responsible for widespread fears about family planning. Everywhere I traveled, family planning workers told me about the impact of rumors in hindering acceptance of contraceptives. The tales that circulate are sometimes extravagant. In Kenya, for example, I was told that "there was a woman who got sick and had to be operated on. They opened her brain and found her IUD." Such rumors were legion in all the countries I visited. I was also to hear that "once you take the pill you will become sterile," and "pills produce deformed children."

Superstitions also influence women who might otherwise wish to use a family planning method. Outside Kankesanturai in Sri Lanka, a forty-year-old rural Hindu woman — already the mother of eight children — told me she did not need family planning methods because she was sure she would only bear nine children, adding, "my horoscope says so."

75

Given the range of problems that some women do experience with contraceptive methods they have tried to use, it is little wonder that unfounded tales arise. Bleeding, infection, dizziness, backaches, and headaches were mentioned repeatedly as side effects of contraceptives. Once a woman tells another of any such symptoms, rumors and fears are set loose. Women told me: "Pills made me sick"; "I had an IUD and lost it so I became pregnant"; or "The IUD made me bleed a lot, so now I'm anemic." Only a handful of women said, "I'm fine," or "I have no problem with my IUD."

In my conversations with family planning workers and medical personnel, I also learned of the stigma attached to the use of the condom. Known to be used by men when they visit prostitutes, it is considered unsuitable by both men and women for use in conjugal relations. On the other hand, I also heard much about male opposition to women's use of contraceptives; many men think that their wives would take advantage of their freedom from pregnancy to have relations with other men.

Some women expressed genuine anger to me about the fact that family planning programs and techniques generally tend to concentrate only on women: "Why do *women* have to use all the contraceptives? Why don't *men* start, too?" One woman pointed her finger at me, saying: "Be sure to go back and tell the U.N. that men, too, should use contraceptives; they should invent a pill for men."

Another factor, the lack of communication between members of a couple, was mentioned time and again as a serious barrier to family planning — by the women I interviewed and by the doctors and other staff members of family planning programs.

Especially in rural areas, subjects relating to intimate relations are rarely discussed by husbands and wives. Each member of the couple often remains ignorant of the other's thoughts and attitudes about family size. If a wife needs her husband's consent to use a contraceptive, but dares not ask, the barrier remains.

Where communication between husbands and wives remains difficult, it is certainly also a possibility that some husbands, too, may look favorably upon limiting the number of births in the family, but may feel reluctant to discuss the issue with their wives. Family planning workers and doctors repeatedly stressed that sex education in schools, at a very early age, is absolutely necessary if this communication gap between husband and wife is to be closed. "Many young people do not even know where a child comes from."

In Egypt, a social worker in Alexandria emphasized the importance of sex education, saying that it is vitally important not only for family planning, but also for the quality of the couple's communication and understanding. Now thirty-five, she had met her husband while she was a student at the school of social work and had been married at twenty-two. She was from a family of eleven children and said that her own mother had been given away by her parents in a traditional marriage at the age of fourteen. She herself was proud to have been allowed to have a courtship before her marriage. When I asked about her work in the field of family planning, she said:

"It is not the women who are against family planning. Mostly men are the ones who oppose it. There are many differences among classes, too. For instance, even educated couples think that a boy is a very important person in the family because he carries on the family's name. So they want to have children until they get a boy. In the poorer classes, they think, 'Well, Allah wants it, so how could I prevent it?'"

When I asked this social worker whether she thought religious beliefs were a barrier to family planning, she replied:

"No, it's the husbands' own beliefs that are a problem—not those of the religious leaders. But you see, all people should have training in parenthood, since both men and women must know about sex and learn how to raise their children. Our schools do not give girls, in particular, any idea about sex education, and the parents — even the mothers — think that talking to girls on such a subject is prohibited; that's why the girls go into this blind. For the husband, the most important thing is the sexual relationship, but even the men don't know much about sexual relations. It comes by experience. Unless he has had experience before he marries, he will know nothing about it, and both of them will be in the same situation. Then they do not get on well."

One young woman in a fishing village in Sri Lanka went so far as to say that she feared marriage itself, because she might not be able to communicate properly with her future husband and convince him to limit the number of births in their family. After ten years of schooling, she had found work helping several women friends organize a cooperative produce store. She spoke with assurance and a sense of independence and said that she hoped she would find a husband who had also left the land, since she did not want to till the soil like her parents. But there was another dimension to her concern about the qualities of a future husband:

"I'm very much afraid of marriage. My married friends, after a certain time, complain and say they are not happy. The couple doesn't get along together because they don't really talk to each other as they should. Most women, once they have a certain number of children, think they should stop. The woman says 'enough,' but the man doesn't care. It is not his problem. The man wants sex, and the children continue to come. After a while, the woman refuses relations out of fear of having more children. Then the man goes and has sex outside. Men must understand what women's lives are like. They must be taught."

Also in Sri Lanka, Dr. Herat of the Child and Maternal Health Office elaborated on his view that women's submissiveness and silence were the major barriers to the family planning programs he had witnessed.

"Women are very modest. When the husband comes home, he may be drunk — and then the wife doesn't dare say anything. So he has relations with her, and she becomes pregnant because she does not dare

77

resist him. And these women will not tell their husbands, 'We are having too many children. We can't look after them when they're sick or when they are grown.' They never say that."

Dr. Herat explained that traditional fertility values are also important. Women feel obliged by traditional role patterns to bear children, whether or not the family can provide for them.

"And what happens when a child is not produced within, say, twelve or fourteen months? People say, 'The woman is barren; send that woman away.' The blame falls upon the woman. Male dominance is a very important factor in this country."

It is an enormously important factor elsewhere as well. In southern Sudan, Dr. Shahata, a male gynecologist, told me that many women in that region are divorced because they have not borne children. Dr. Shahata explained that much of the high incidence of infertility there is due to filaria and venereal disease, which can be carried by men as well as women, but that if he asks the husbands to have a seminal analysis, they refuse. In that culture, too, the inability to have a child is automatically assumed to be the woman's fault.

When I asked Maria Luisa—the Zapotec Indian woman I spoke with in southern Mexico—if the men of her village would permit their wives to control the number of pregnancies, she laughed at my question:

"Heavens, no! They say terrible things about women who want to. Some say, 'The only reason you want birth control is so you can go with other men.' Once the radio said, 'Father of the family, if you want to give your children a good upbringing, take care of them well and remember that small families live better.' Well, my brother just laughed. You see, some people are very ignorant."

Dr. Hernandez, the young director of the hospital in Dolores Hidalgo, Mexico, told me that he believed the male attitude of machismo is the biggest barrier to family planning acceptance. Religious attitudes sometimes also are a hindrance, he said, but generally that is because of the local priest's convictions, not because of the religious attitudes of the family.

"Often the husband doesn't give anything to the wife or he doesn't take care of the family, but when the wife wants to do something to prevent a pregnancy, he will get angry and will beat her because she is going against all the social trends.

"The man thinks that the woman is taking a view that reverses her sex role — that she is trying to attain his own status in sex relations by claiming a say in whether *she* wants to have a child or not. Before, it was the *man* who was the only one to say when and how, and now the woman also wants the capacity to decide. This is looked upon as going against her husband's virility.

"As for religion, its importance in this connection varies. Just one week ago, a woman came and said that she wanted to have her IUD removed because she wanted to take communion in church. The priest had told her that if she had an IUD he would not give her the sacrament."

A little later, as I interviewed a woman in her forties outside Dr. Hernandez's office, I was told a similar story when I asked this woman whether or not she attends mass.

"Yes. The only thing I *don't* do is go to confession, because then I would have to confess that I take the pill, and the priest would say, 'Leave the church.' I could still go to mass, but he wouldn't give me holy communion if I told about the pill."

In Mombasa, Kenya, I met with a family planning worker, Mary Mwado, who has worked in the population field for many years. She met me for lunch in a downtown restaurant one Sunday — accompanied by her husband, who respectfully listened while she told me about some of the problems she encounters in her work:

"We get referrals from other workers. A nutritionist, for example, will come and tell us that she visited a home and feels that the home needs advice on family planning. So we go to the family and talk with them. We also go the child welfare clinic and talk with mothers there. We find that some do not feel free to talk about their problems there, so we go to their own homes and have further discussions. The woman might say, 'I'm willing to practice family planning, but my husband is against it. I've tried to persuade him, but he has refused. So I don't know whether there is anything you can do for me.'"

I asked Mary Mwado what reasons the men give for their opposition to family planning.

"Some say that they are able to care for their children—so they don't see why they should participate in family planning. Others say they don't see why they should plan their families, since the idea is not an African tradition but has been brought in by Westerners. Also, some men fear that when a woman starts using family planning, she is in that way exposed to the world and can go with any other man, since she knows she won't get pregnant. They don't trust their wives."

Mary Mwado's words were echoed by a group of women I later met in the same town. All were members of local service organizations and thus represented the educated and concerned women of the area. As we discussed barriers to family planning, they explained that superstition, fear, and their husbands' attitudes — as well as polygamy — are the important factors that relate to the family planning issue in their region. One woman told me, "Women fear medicines and they fear their husbands. There are a lot of fears, and it will take much time to catch on." A second woman added:

"The men don't understand that family planning is good because it gives the woman time to rest between pregnancies. They don't care much about that, or about the condition of their children. You'll never see a man going to a family planning clinic. The men here believe: Let a woman be free of childbearing and she will go everywhere. They want a woman to have a child every year until she becomes old, while they are free to go gadding about. So if a woman doesn't keep on having children, her husband will get angry and take another wife."

My conversations with rural women persuaded me that—in contrast to their relatively free resort to folk "remedies," such as those described by the Tunisian woman quoted earlier—they rarely feel free to decide to use *modern* contraceptive methods on their own, *without* the approval of their menfolk. If they use such methods, it is either because they have obtained the consent of their husbands, or because the leaders of their nation have urged people to plan their families. If the latter is true, women can then say to their husbands: "The President told us to do it." This was the case in Tunisia, where President Bourguiba repeatedly had taken a public stand on the importance of parental responsibility toward children, and thus the advantages of family planning.

A nomad woman I met in a public health clinic near Sfax, Tunisia, told me that she had had ten children and then had obtained an IUD despite her husband's objections. When I asked why he had objected, she said:

"My husband used to say that it isn't normal to avoid a life that you are destined to have. He said that if I had been given a potential to bear a certain number of children, it was necessary to bring them into the world. He said I didn't have the right to prevent it—that I was like a chicken with a certain number of eggs to lay, and that I had to lay them. He said it would be a sin not to.

"My husband at first didn't know that I had an IUD. I didn't want any more children. My health wouldn't stand it. Now he agrees because they talk about it on the radio."

In Le Kef, Tunisia, I talked one morning with another nomad woman who was still propped up in her bed in the family planning clinic, having undergone a tubal ligation the day before. She said she was relieved that now she could not get pregnant again; she was thirty-five years old and did not want any more children. Her husband is a shepherd, and the family follows the herd of sheep in a seasonal search for grass. They pitch their tent wherever they find water.

"I was married at thirteen," she told me. "I had just reached puberty. Now I have five children. The youngest is three years old. I had eleven children in all — six others died. Two were stillborn, and the others died before they were a year old."

Although Tunisia has a relatively well-organized and well-staffed medical infrastructure, this woman—because she follows her husband and the herds from one end of the country to the other — had little experience with health-care services. She was visibly nervous about our visit—the hospital surroundings were unfamiliar to her, and this was the first time she had ever been in a bed. I asked her whether a midwife had been present at the births of her children.

"Sometimes, yes, but sometimes I was alone. The last time, I had complications. The child just wouldn't come out. The head came out and then went back in again. Finally, they decided to take me to the hospital, but I gave birth on the way. The baby was already dead, so I turned around and went home."

I asked this young woman how long she generally nursed her children.

"About two and a half years," she replied. "I wanted to have this operation because I can't care for more children. We are too poor. Before, all the babies were dying. I was afraid to stop having children because I thought they might all die. I want my children to have lots of things, and I want them to have a good place in life, but my husband doesn't agree with these things. My daughters have never been to school. Only one son has attended school, and he has to change each time we move again."

I asked what her husband thought about her operation to prevent new pregnancies. He had agreed to it, she told me, and then added, "But he wanted me to wait until summer was over, so I could help in the fields.

"I guess all the women of the world have these same problems. I just don't understand my life. I have nothing to wish for. I am here—that is all. Life doesn't serve any purpose at all."

When I questioned the woman further, I found that she had never heard about family planning or contraceptives. She had only heard that there was "an operation." A cousin had told her about it.

Confronted with increasing economic pressures, malnutrition, and poor health, the women with whom I spoke expressed the hope that their children would have a better life than their own. Many felt that if they had fewer children, they would be able to give them more food, clothing, education — and attention. Yet many among them felt caught in a "vicious circle" of powerlessness to do anything about it. Their ability to improve the lives of their families is stymied on several fronts. It is limited by their legal status, their lack of income-earning skills, their restricted mobility, the shortage of sensitively managed health services, and—as women repeatedly told me—by the unwillingness of their men to use or allow the women themselves to use contraceptives. Another factor in the "vicious circle" is the limited degree of personal autonomy allowed them—their lack of freedom to participate in the decisions that govern their lives.

At a health clinic in Villagran, Mexico, I found twenty-five women waiting for the medical consultations to begin. Among them was a small, slim woman, dressed in pants and a blouse, who volunteered to talk with me once the group discussion ended. The woman's three-year-old daughter and a smaller child, barely old enough to stand, were with her. Throughout our conversation, the children waited patiently while their mother told of her dilemma. She was nineteen years old, married to a tradesman, and said she knew how to read and write "just a little." She explained that her widower father had been very poor and that she had started working at the age of ten in order to help raise her five brothers and sisters.

"I went to school for a while, but the teacher didn't come to school very often, so we didn't learn much. I guess I taught myself to read.

"I have been married for four years. I have only these two children. The first is three, the other almost a year."

I interrupted the young woman, recalling that earlier, when we had talked in the group with the other women, several of them had said that one of the main changes they had witnessed in the last few generations was the greater availability of education. I asked her whether she thought other important changes had taken place.

"The main thing that makes the times different, I think, is the control women have over the number of children in a family. A family can be planned now; it can live a better life. Women have more facilities for everything because of this. I began to take contraceptives when this last child was eight months old. I take the pill.

"My husband wants a boy because these children are both girls; he doesn't know that I am taking the pill. He wants a boy and says that when I have one, then I can use contraceptives. I want to wait at least two years so that this little girl is older. Then I will try for the boy."

The fact that this young woman controlled her pregnancies without her husband's knowledge made her quite exceptional among the women I interviewed. Unlike many of the rural women I spoke with, however, she had the advantage of being able to act on her decision with relatively little risk of "being found out" — since she could easily obtain birth control information and supplies while taking her children to the nearby general health clinic. I asked her if she and her husband ever talked with one another about her carefully thought-out reasons for spacing their children.

"No, almost never. In fact, my husband has a sister who is using a contraceptive method. She asked me if I was interested in using one, and I said 'no' because I didn't want her to tell my husband. He might find out that I already use them. I just want to wait a few years and rest. When I wanted the pills, I came here to the health center. I keep them in the kitchen. When I'm cooking dinner, I take a pill and he doesn't notice. Either that or I take one while he is sleeping. But all this is very dangerous, you know, because my husband went to school; he is smart. He knows about such things. One time he did find them and I was terribly frightened. I had hidden them in a closet, under some clothes. He found them and asked, "What are these pills?' I just said that my baby daughter had found them and brought them into the house. I told him I took them away from her because she was going to eat them. My husband told me, 'You know, these pills are very dangerous because they are for not having children. If I find out that you are taking them, you will see what I will do to you!' He threatened to hit me. For me, family planning is very important because my husband does not earn big wages. For the moment, we just can't afford more than two children."

When I asked the young mother what she wanted most for her children in later life, she told me — with equal fervor — what I had already heard from many other mothers and was to hear from many more. Like the others, she, too, recalled her own childhood in her answer:

"I told you we were very poor when I was a child. We were six children, and my father didn't earn much. That is why I want just two or three children. I don't want my children to grow up like me—without an education. I feel very ashamed and bad about not having any education. I want my children to go to school and learn many, many things. I don't want them to live by the rumors of the street. I want them to learn for themselves. I want them to be independent and proud of themselves."

# 6

LEARNING, WORK, AND ASPIRATIONS

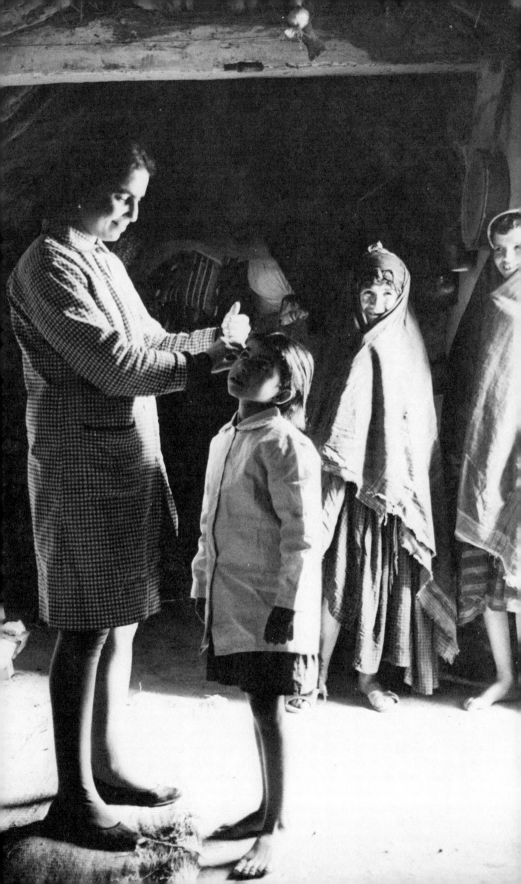

# "I want to learn to help other people"

## LEARNING, WORK, AND ASPIRATIONS

Hands folded primly on their knees, seventeen young women in starched white uniforms sat waiting on a bench outside the Juba hospital one Sunday morning. They were members of the different tribes of southern Sudan, sent to Juba to study midwifery. Few among them were literate. Their only qualification was that the chiefs of their tribes had selected them for the training program. They would return to their home villages after two years of training in conducting normal deliveries and learning the elements of hygiene, nutrition, and infant care.

The bustle of hospital activities continued around us, but the young women paid little attention to the comings and goings of patients and doctors. They sat proudly, waiting for me to speak. Once I had explained the nature of my visit and had requested volunteers for individual conversations, several students raised their hands to say they would be willing to talk with me about their families and their future plans.

The first young woman I spoke with, a twenty-six-year-old member of the Zande tribe, had been married at eighteen to a man who had two other wives. She had divorced him, even though she was a Catholic, "because he beat me often." When I asked why she had come to the midwife school, she replied:

"I wanted to become a midwife because my father and mother are old. My brothers and sisters have not been to school. They are only digging in the field. I thought it would be good to become a midwife so I could help my parents by earning a wage. I met some girls who had taken this course, and I saw that they learned good things. Also, if someone becomes a midwife, it will help the country. That's why I have chosen it. Now I can help my country."

I asked the young woman how her life was different from her mother's.

"The difference is that I have become cleaner than she is. I used to work hard digging outside and doing everything in the house. I would get all dirty. But I didn't know about hygiene or how to clean myself. Now I know. I will go back to my tribe and teach other women. They have enough water, but they have no knowledge."

I asked her what she thought the women of her tribe needed most to learn. "Women want to learn the new things in health, how best to dig and do the work in the field or vegetable garden and in the house," she replied. "They want to learn about foods and cooking. I will try my best to teach them." When I asked what work she would have liked to have chosen had she been able to go to school, she told me: "I would have been a teacher — a teacher to help educate others."

The words of this Sudanese woman echoed those of many of the less educated women I interviewed in Sudan and in the other countries I visited. When they spoke of "education" for themselves, they usually had non-formal training in mind as the primary means of improving their existence in the immediate future. When they spoke of "education" for their children, they meant formal schooling, believing that the opportunity to learn would automatically provide their children with the opportunity to earn in the future. "I must learn new skills or I will be left behind and my family will suffer," they told me. "My children must not remain ignorant like me." Many also expressed their desire to "be able to understand what goes on," "to be able to communicate better with others," "to keep up with my husband," and "to be able to help others."

At the Juba hospital, I talked about education and work with a second midwife student. She was twenty-seven years old, unmarried, and had never attended school. She had learned to read "a little" from her brother, who was the only literate member of the family.

"I have four brothers and four sisters, but they are from different mothers — my father had two wives. I never went to school, but I have a brother who attends the university in Khartoum. When I heard about this training school, I wanted to come here. My mother wanted me to come also, but my father was reluctant.

"My life will be different from my mother's. Before, people had plenty of everything. Now they have to have cash to buy things. I will know everything better than my mother. I can work and get money and buy things to help her in her house—show her how to better care for our house. I will earn money after I learn to deliver babies and to care for them and their mothers — after I learn to help other women.

"I want to learn to teach women to look after their children, to boil water, and to take care of the older people. That is what they need most. When I have children, I will treat them all the same. Both girls and boys will go to school. I want them to have an education."

Apart from being a basic need essential to self-esteem and a sense of self-worth, education and "keeping up with the times" is crucial to the development process — to securing the welfare and participation of citizens.

The issue of the relevance of education to improved welfare — the question of "education for what?"— was a problem emphasized by many of the women leaders I interviewed. Often, it seems, national educational systems were styled after those of the former colonial powers. Yet the colonial system of education was designed to train native clerks and minor officials to serve in the colonial administration. It hardly encouraged the education of leaders to manage national or local affairs. Thus in many poor countries that have become independent in recent years, educational systems have yet to be redesigned to serve real and immediate national and local needs.

Speaking of their own educational needs, some rural women told me they would rather learn how to improve their crops than learn how to read. Successful crops were necessary for survival, they said; reading was not. This is not to say that the women with whom I spoke do not want literacy programs; many explicitly said they want such training. But these women know that they need first to meet their families' most critical, immediate needs, and their responses pointed to one of the problem areas of educational "relevance": the usefulness of existing literacy training programs to meeting everyday needs.

As I listened to poor rural women in different countries and regions speak about their many *specific* learning requirements, I found that they were interested in training or education for two basic reasons. First, they want to improve the health of their families, for which they seek *knowledge* and *skills* pertinent to cultivation, nutrition, hygiene, and health care. And second, they seek training in *remunerable skills* in order to earn the cash necessary to improve the health and economic situation of their families and to send their children to school.

Whenever I asked rural women what they would most like to learn if they had the opportunity, they invariably named several health-related skills: improved ways of growing food for family subsistence, nutrition, cooking, hygiene, health care, budgeting, and family planning. In addition, they wanted skills that would enable them to earn cash: sewing, handicrafts, new agricultural techniques, and some accounting and marketing skills.

Many of the women I met spoke of training and education as tools to help them emerge from poverty. When, for example, I asked Sophia, the Zapotec Indian woman I interviewed in southern Mexico, what she would have chosen to learn had she been able to go to school, she replied, "I don't know *what* exactly, but it would have been something that would earn money. We are very backward here and we don't know anything."

The interpreter, a woman who was familiar with the life and work routines of the women of the region, balked at Sophia's words of self-deprecation, saying, "That is not true — you know lots of things: you know how to farm, how to cook, how to raise small animals. You know many things."

Sophia shook her head in disagreement and replied, "But the problem is that we don't know how to *earn money*."

Uppermost in the minds of the women who wanted training to enable them to earn cash was the welfare of their children. In Maskeliya, Sri Lanka, a thirty-nine-year-old housewife and mother of six children was one of the many women I spoke with who daily struggle to make ends meet and to assure the education of their children. She told me she knew how to read a little because she had attended school until she was ten years old. Her husband finds occasional work in a local hotel, she said, but his intermittent earnings are not enough to provide for eight people.

"We don't have enough to eat — and it is because we have such a large family. But somehow I manage. My father earns a bit of cash, and an uncle works in a laundry and gives me a little money each month. This way I am able to buy schoolbooks for my children. I may be having a lot of troubles now, but I am determined to give my children an education so they won't be in the same kind of situation I am in. My life is not very easy."

Asked what she would study if she were able to attend a training course at this point in her life, the woman replied, "Oh, if there was an opportunity like that I would certainly take up sewing. I could then make garments and sell them. I would be able to earn some money and see to it that the children, at least, come out well in life."

In a remote village of Kenya, I met an illiterate, young peasant woman who had just turned seventeen. She works the land with her husband and lives on a cooperative plantation. We had driven through fields and gullies for many miles before reaching the isolated settlement in which she lived. The village — a cluster of thatch-roofed homes — was hidden among high stalks of sugar cane and, I learned, was visited by government extension workers only once or twice a month.

The young woman had never attended school and had left the settlement only a few times to travel to the nearest market town. She had married at fifteen and had no children yet, but she said, "I would like to have four." She hoped her children would have a better life than hers— if only they could have an education. She, too, wanted to help others.

"I would like my children to get enough education. Women, you know, have more talents for doing things than men. It's only that men's talents are better recognized because they only concentrate on a few things. Women have got so many things to do that nobody ever looks at how many things they do. If I had a chance to learn something, I would like to learn how to help people. I would like to be a nurse."

In a women's training center in central Tunisia, I talked with a semiliterate woman of twenty-five as we sat in the office of the center's director. A closed door did not altogether keep out the hum of students at work in the next room or the hot spring air of Tunisia's Sahel. Although she had volunteered to speak with me, the young woman appeared nervous about our conversation. She rocked back and forth on her straight-backed chair as she told her story and added her views on the importance of education and training. Her father, she said, had a small farm, and the family was very poor.

"I have seven brothers and sisters at home. I came here because I don't want to lead a life like my mother's. I want to have knowledge. My mother had a disagreeable life because my father held her under his thumb. He had great authority over her because she had no education. If I can get an education, I will be more at ease than she was.

"I have come back here for the second time. I never went to school, so I am trying to learn something here at the center. My father didn't want me to come. He listens to those around him and is influenced by them. For example, they say, 'Why send a daughter to school? We aren't accustomed to sending girls to school to have their eyes opened, and to know what happens in the cities. They must continue to stay with their eyes closed.' My father can read Arabic, but he is learned only in the Koran's teachings.

"My mother would have had a greater influence on me if she had been educated. She would have helped all of us. But she can't teach us anything because she is so ignorant. And my father, too, would have been more understanding if he had had more education. He would have sent us to school. He wouldn't have let us grow up like this without any schooling.

"If I were ever in a position of responsibility, I would be sure that women had access to education. That is what they need first of all — education. Women have need of health education, hygiene education, and family planning. They have to learn how to take care of their children.

"I would like to be like those young women who are well-educated, who have learned French and Arabic, who know how to read well. That's what I would like. Of course, there are women who are educated and those who aren't, but we are all women just the same. Women are just as capable as men, and I hope that women—through their education—will come to be more equal to men. That way they would be like them, think like them, and work for the same goals.

"In a couple, education and culture are the most essential things. If both are educated and learned, they will please each other, be closer to each other. I want my daughters to go very far with their education. I want them to work and to have a good future. I have learned to read a bit here, but I want to learn so much more. I want to know about *everything*."

When we left the center a few hours later, the interpreter told me that several days before, the young trainee had been found peeling labels off the canned goods stored in the kitchen. Having no access to books—or to money with which to buy them—she collected the labels in order to practice her reading. It mattered little to her that the words on the labels listed only the ingredients of a soup.

Nearly every uneducated woman I encountered—whether she lived in a rural or urban area—expressed a similar yearning for education. Yet, as the conversations presented in earlier chapters reveal, a woman's will to participate (or to learn) is not always enough; she must be *permitted* to learn, to have the freedom to go where the learning is taking place. All too often, the opportunity to do that depends on a father's or a husband's consent.

Maggie Gona, a prominent social worker in Mombasa, Kenya, stressed the importance of male encouragement when she spoke of the educational needs of women in the Mombasa area.

"Encouragement from our husbands is very, very important. The husbands should not think that because they are heads of families they have all the rights. They must listen to their wives. Whatever women have achieved in this world, they say, has been possible because of the kind of togetherness between a man and a woman.

"We must start to plan with women. We must start with what they know and then build on to what they need, because if you are bringing change all of a sudden, you will confuse women and you will not win the objective you seek. What I believe they need first is education. It is the key to everything, even for the women who are no longer young. We are lucky to have adult education in Kenya. This is very important. Even if she is not educated, a woman has *hands*. She can make a small amount of money with handicrafts, using the local materials here. She can sell them to a shop and get paid for them. Then she can buy food for her children. Through education, exchanging ideas, and learning new angles, our women—educated or uneducated—can achieve what they want."

Maggie Gona's statement expressed the theoretical and optimistic side of the coin. Many of the educated women with whom I spoke told of the resistance women in fact encounter when they attempt to learn, or to work outside the home. Traditional attitudes of women's "place" continue to prevent participation in training programs or, thereafter, in the labor force.

In Egypt, I discussed these problems with Zahia Marzouk, who, in addition to serving as president of the Family Planning Association of Alexandria, is also a sculptress, painter, social worker — and former government official. As we sat in the garden outside her office, she willingly voiced opinions formed in over forty years of social work experience. When I asked what she considered to be the principal barriers to women's advancement in Egypt, she very candidly replied:

"Well, *men*. Men still don't understand that a woman can do something valuable—especially after she gets married. They think that after she gets married, she's no good. She must sit down and cook and take care of her children and take care of her husband. They think she should do nothing, even if she is educated. Why should you educate a girl in a university and then keep her inside the house? It's ridiculous! Her ability is put in prison."

In a village sixty miles south of Alexandria, a young woman I interviewed provided an example of the problems facing women who want to work. Having completed her secondary-school education, the young woman was attending a commercial course offered miles from her home. Covered by a long, black veil, she traveled by train for an hour each morning to reach the distant school. That she was allowed the freedom to do so was a source of pride to her. She appeared pleased to have the occasion to talk with a foreign visitor and spoke about her parents with admiration and appreciation. But the story of what she expected of her life after marriage was unsettling.

"I am seventeen years old and I attend the second year of a commercial school. This is quite different from the life of my mother. She is illiterate and was married in the traditional manner [to a man she did not know and had not seen] at age fifteen. I am one of five children in the family. My father is a grocer. My parents are very close to one another, and they take good care of us. Even though my mother was uneducated, she helped her husband and was a good mother to us.

"I am engaged to be married. I don't know my fiancé well, but I was allowed to speak with him the day he came to ask for my hand. My parents asked me if I wanted him, and I said yes. I would not have agreed to it if I didn't like him. He has a university education and is in the army."

I asked the young woman what qualities she hoped for in her husband, and whether she was going to continue to study and to work after her marriage.

"I would like my husband to be religious, to take care of his household, to care for his wife, to work well, and to serve his country.

"My fiancé wants me to continue my studies, but he doesn't want me to work. I would like to, but my fiancé says, 'If one day we need your work, then you can; but if we don't need it, no.' You see, here, when girls finish school, they just go back into the house and don't come out after that. Only rarely are we allowed to go out; but the boys, naturally, are allowed to go out and about. I would have liked to have been a boy so as to do that. And if I had been a boy, I would have liked to work—to earn a good salary, to do a job the country needs.

"I want *my* children to be well-educated, and I want them to have more freedom than I have."

Many women talked to me about the problem of the "double workday" that burdens the lives of both rural and urban women. When a woman does a full day's work outside the household—whether it is unpaid work in the field, producing for family subsistence, or work for pay — she generally returns home to another full day's work of household tasks that traditionally have been the responsibility of women.

In Alexandria, Zahia Marzouk had spoken vehemently about this problem:

"Men are selfish. They do not share in the work of the home. I made a survey on the problems of working mothers, and I found that very few men — 1.3 men among the husbands of 750 working women — were helping their wives. But they were nevertheless enjoying their wives' salaries. Even if we say that working in the house would impair the dignity of the man, there are tasks that would not touch his dignity. Why shouldn't he do them? Taking the children to school—why shouldn't he do that? Or sitting with his children, helping to revise homework? Sometimes the wife even pays half the rent. *Why* should the man share in her income and not join in helping her do her 'duty' when she is working outside the home as much as he is?"

Amina Saïd, director of the Egyptian publishing house, Al Hilal, expressed the working woman's problem in yet another way:

"Do you know what I would choose for a statue of a national hero in this country? The working woman. The working woman is the national hero because she goes to school and then goes to a university and graduates. She works too — takes a job. She works exactly like a man. Even in the fields, the peasant woman works beside the husband, seven hours a day at hard work. Then she goes home and is required to play the role of housewife 100 per cent — cooking, cleaning, washing, caring for the children. A woman does two major jobs, which any man would never be able to do."

In Mexico, sociologist Maria del Carmen Elu de Lenero also acknowledged the problem of the double day, noting that: "Most of the women who are working at this time have no choice about whether to work or not. They *have* to work, because if they don't the children won't eat." She added, however, that even if women are in the labor market because of economic necessity rather than choice, their increasing economic independence is "one of the most important factors of change" in the world today.

Many of the professional women I interviewed spoke of the difficulties that women encounter in the work place itself. Discriminatory practices and attitudes, humiliation, child-care difficulties, male opposition, and unequal pay were just some of their complaints. They insisted that women must know their rights as individuals and strive to gain self-confidence as part of their preparation for work.

Victoria Yar Arol, the twenty-nine-year-old member of the People's Regional Assembly of Southern Sudan, told me of her concern for women who work:

"You see, our constitution grants women equal rights in all walks of life — equal pay for equal work, equal job opportunity, and so on. But there are times when there are people who exploit the ignorance of our women. Not many of our women know what is in the constitution because not many of them are educated. And even the few who are educated do not know the importance of knowing what is in the constitution. For example, the constitution grants women freedom to participate with men in every aspect of life. Yet if this right is infringed upon, women don't know how to fight for it. They don't *know* their rights.

"I'll give you an example that is rather sensitive. It is a woman's right to be employed in a government department. Sometimes, however, the authorities or the head of that department may use the job as if it were a favor for a certain woman. The department head may want to make the woman feel that the job was not given to her because it is her right, but only because he arranged it so. He is exploiting the woman—getting her in so that he can play with her. If a woman knows that she's employed on her own rights and on her own merits, the man will not be able to bother her."

Fatma Zohra, a social worker in the northern Tunisian town of Le Kef, expressed to me her frustration about yet another very difficult barrier to women's participation in and contribution to the work force: the limitation imposed upon her and other women by social custom.

Fatma Zohra is unmarried and in her twenties. Even though she has lived in Le Kef most of her life and is a senior staff member of the Ministry of Social Welfare there, she nevertheless cannot attend evening meetings or social gatherings. If she were a man or accompanied by a husband, there would be no barrier to her participation. She stated that the reluctance to accept her as a professional comes especially from the men:

"I have always felt a hesitation on their part because I can't go to or do things as a man can. It is still a very traditional milieu in which we live here. Perhaps if I were married it would be different, but as a single woman it is very difficult. I am inclined to agree that a man would be better off in this position. They have just promoted a man ahead of me, and I think this is best. He is more free to come and go than I am. It will be easier for him."

Barriers to the participation of women in the work force on an equal basis with men exist in rural areas as well. In Kenya, for example, many rural women told me that it is easier for men to obtain credit for agricultural or business ventures than it is for women. Credit institutions rarely extend credit to women, since in many cases, women do not hold title to the land they till.

In Machakos, Kenya, the leader of a women's cooperative told me:

"The women here are trying to do something for themselves. The problem is that when they start something, they don't have any capital and it is very difficult. They do many things to get money of their own. Some of them are folk dancers, and they perform at public occasions. Others are involved in building a nursery school for cooperative day-care. Still others have opened shops. It all started when we were given plots of land. We started talking and thought that if we formed a group we could create a park. We built it, and from that time on we had the feeling that we could work together. We also thought about crafts that would bring money, and we found a place to sell our work. It started like that. After one project was finished, we started another."

This woman's account of how women had begun to work together on self-help projects in her town echoed similar tales I had heard from women in other countries. Like the other women concerned about cooperative work, the Machakos businesswoman commented, "But what women need most of all, I think, is education. Take me, for example. In my work, I need to be able to count, but I don't know how to very well. It is difficult for me. To make any progress, women need to have an education."

Contrary to the expectations of many rural women with whom I spoke, however, education or skills do not necessarily guarantee the opportunity to earn a wage. In Sri Lanka, for example, chronic unemployment affects women as well as men. Since 1945, the small island country has provided free education from kindergarten through university to all who qualify. Yet Sri Lankans are finding that even a university education does not guarantee employment.

Malsiré Dias, a Sri Lankan sociologist, told me that university graduates in her country encounter enormous difficulties in finding jobs:

"You see, there is almost an equal number of girls and boys getting a secondary education. In higher education, too, it is the same. For instance, at the medical faculty this year, the ratio was 50-50. I think it was similar for other faculties. This has had a tremendous influence on attitudinal change, because students return to the rural areas with new ideas, new aspirations, and a great desire to enter the job market. Some of them succeed."

These young Sri Lankan university graduates go back to their villages, I was told, because:

"They can't afford to stay in the city. This is the trouble — the economic factor and unemployment. They can't find jobs here, and they can't live in the city without earning money. Even the trained young people, with a good education, are forced to stay in the village and look for a break. But there is no employment in the village for them. There is this problem of the well-educated unemployed — and it is the same for men and women.

"But, then again, in Sri Lanka education is valued for its own sake. It is deeply valued. Even the traditional Ceylonese songs are always advising the young to be educated. Education for education's sake. We have the highest literacy rate in this region of the world — 80 per cent."

One of the problems facing Sri Lanka is the emigration of its educated young. There are some 25,000 Sri Lankans living in the London area alone. Women, however, are reluctant to emigrate — unless they are married and accompany their husbands.

The president of the Sri Lanka Association of University Women, Dorothy Abeywickreme, received me in her office at the Ceylon Tobacco Company, where she holds an executive position. She has been active in the AUW for many years and is pleased to see Sri Lankan women preparing for a variety of professions. However, she too emphasized that young women university graduates encounter great difficulties when searching for employment. She told me that the AUW had just received a grant to enable it to teach typing to 7,000 women graduates who otherwise would not find employment.

In Mombasa, Kenya, a group of women leaders discussed with me their views on the training needs of women in their area. They had gathered to plan their collective participation in the Mombasa Agricultural Show.

Each woman represented a different religious group, voluntary organization, or government agency. In all, five women contributed to the conversation, during which they stressed the need to carefully "think through" educational programs for all ages. If this is not done, they said, "education serves no purpose." "We want to teach women crafts so they can earn money," they said, "but it is difficult for them to come and learn since they have so many duties at home. And, in the town here, the women are very isolated."

One woman who had introduced herself as a social worker was a Moslem and had shrugged off her long black veil as we sat talking. Responding to my question about the needs of women in the Mombasa area, she replied:

"They need to learn how to care for their homes, to cook, and to manage a budget. The budget is the most important thing. Take the case of a woman whose husband earns about 300 shillings [U.S. $42] and who comes to you and says, 'I have a problem with my husband. He doesn't want to give me money. I need this and that. Can you help me?' And then you look into it and find that the woman has created her own problem because she cannot budget."

"I think something ought to be done here in Kenya," another woman added, "so that women could be given a chance. Most of the time *they* are the providers. You see, in the rural areas, women have plots of land, and if you've got a plot, you can get food from it. In town, there are no plots of land, so if your husband is earning about 200 shillings [U.S. $28] and you would like to supplement that by working, then there should be a way to let you do that. The other problem is that women are sewing or embroidering to earn money. They stitch, make tablecloths, and then they have no market. I think women need to be educated as to what is needed in the market.

"First, we should investigate the market, see what is needed, and only then should we teach them to make what is needed. You see, they get discouraged and say, 'Why should I go waste my time if nobody buys what I make?' So the problem lies with the leaders. Before you start a group, you must find a market and investigate what things can be sold and where they can be sold. Also, the men buy from the women and then sell for much more in the market. Our women should be educated to become businesswomen."

"Nothing is properly organized," another woman added. "That is the problem. Also, if there were ways of controlling the handicrafts so that the men would not come into the field — as middlemen — then the women really would become their own proprietors throughout Kenya. There would be no men to undercut their work and their earnings. Now, though, the middlemen are making a fantastic profit. They are exploiters — they are doing everything to make themselves rich by undercutting the women. But who is going to educate the women to take this over? Who is going to help the women so that whatever they do, it will be for themselves, and the money will be plowed back instead of going to the middlemen?"

The social worker in the group agreed with the need for organized markets and then turned to the question of employment:

"I think the government has to create more employment for youth also. It seems to be quite a sad story. A student may be educated up to fifteen or sixteen years of age and then when he or she finishes, the chances of getting employment are slim."

Another woman spoke up, observing: "We don't educate students as we should. When they have finished their studies, they don't seem to know anything apart from reading books. The time allocated to practical things is not enough to make anything out of them."

Concern for the education of children was a subject raised by practically all of the women I talked with in the six countries. The advantages of an educated child were often related to the future security of the family and of the child: "They will be able to help the family more in life," or "They will understand the world and be able to work."

In Sri Lanka, Kumari Jayawardene told me that in her country, the major influence on the changing status of women in the past ten or twenty years has been education, and that it has brought other changes as well.

"Socially—through free education—everyone has an equal chance to go to school. Parents don't discriminate between boys and girls as far as their education is concerned, simply because it is free. You just send everyone to school.

"Education has changed attitudes, too. Now many parents *want* their girls to work—because of the extra money they need. And the girls themselves, having earned a degree, of course are not willing to go back to the kitchen—or to start making lace and traditional things. Nor are they going out into the field to help on the farm. They are more ambitious, and they just want ideas on what they can do, so they can cross all the feudal barriers. There's a lot going on. Women are breaking through. Women are not believing in devils any more. They are making their own decisions."

When I asked rural women in the countries I visited whether they thought boys and girls should have equal education — equal access to education — most replied "yes," that children, whether male or female, "should go as far as their abilities can take them." Only a handful thought it was better to educate boys. A few women thought girls should have *more* education because they "care more about their parents," or "care more about people and can help them," and because "women must become leaders."

Maria Luisa, the semiliterate Zapotec Indian woman with whom I talked in southern Mexico, had a totally unambiguous opinion on this subject. As she rolled tortillas near the open hearth fire of her home, we talked at length about her family, the changes taking place around her, and the future. When I asked her if she thought boys and girls should be educated equally, she turned toward me with a look of amazement. Almost aggressively, she declared:

"I would educate women *more* than men. Women bear and raise the children—so women prepare the future. How can the future be good if women are ignorant?"

# 7

POLITICAL PARTICIPATION AND LEADERSHIP

# "We need more women representatives — they know the problems"

## POLITICAL PARTICIPATION AND LEADERSHIP

Seated across from me in her Nairobi office, Julia Ojiambo, the gentle-mannered, small, and attractive woman who is Kenya's Assistant Minister for Housing and Social Affairs, identified the factors that she believes influence Kenyan women's involvement in community life and in national affairs today:

"The Kenyan woman is freer now — freer from household confinement and more confident. She can move outside her home, mix with other women and people from other tribes, and communicate and relate to them. She has gained self-confidence. She can talk to anyone and explain or air her opinion. And this has all come about in the last ten years. Before, women were very shy. You could never get anything out of a Kenyan woman then—she would just sit and look down. You don't see that anymore.

"Now women have realized that there are problems in their homes. And they are very much aware of what they should do to help look for solutions. I'm proud of that. I keep on saying that women are the initiators of our government plans. Really, that is so. Women, in their own way, without even realizing it, will start another school or some project—like better water distribution—simply because they see a need for it. They start farming together because they see the need for easing their labor, or they start knitting and gossiping together, and this is the beginning of a cooperative group. Then, if it is an interesting program, it comes to be discussed in the government's development committee. So I really keep saying that women initiate our policies—and they don't even know that they're doing this.

"As soon as women have the opportunity to play an important role in decision making, they dare participate. They are responding quite quickly, considering the problems they have to overcome for lack of education. They are not prepared. Most of the educated women are still young; we don't yet have educated *older* women. Maybe in ten more years it will be better. The government encourages women to participate, but now women themselves must act."

The rural women with whom I spoke in the six countries generally associated the opportunity to learn and to use their acquired skills in working to help others and to improve the lives of those around them. They said they wanted to participate and "serve the country." Yet when I attempted to draw out their understanding of major issues in the political life of their nations, I found that they had little knowledge of the world beyond the village. They lacked awareness of their legal status, their rights and responsibilities, and the processes that govern their lives. Common barriers to women's involvement in activities outside the home included social class, custom, fear, lack of self-confidence, and insufficient leadership. As many women leaders pointed out, if women are to move on to more participatory roles, they must understand the *mechanics* of participation and become aware of their potential influence on community and national affairs.

Margaret Juan, an employee of the Department of Social Welfare in Juba, Sudan, met with me on the veranda of the town's only hotel. A well-educated woman in her late twenties, she told me she hoped to have an active political career and to serve as one of the "role models" she believes are so important in helping women to gain self-confidence.

Describing the factors that hinder women's involvement in public life, she said:

"We here in southern Sudan have been kept in darkness. A lot of women, especially in the rural areas, know very little. They don't understand. We should tell our women what is happening in other parts of the world and in other parts of the country. You know, women are very courageous—just like men. We have women leaders who step right up, give speeches, or lead demonstrations. If our women see this, it will encourage them. It will make them feel that, after all, we are not still in the past.

"The situation of women at the moment is only a symptom of the general situation of Sudan. There are problems of unemployment, education, and health. The government, or the departments concerned, should help the society so that women, who are part of it, can also be helped. We have many women who are destitute. Poverty dominates their lives. We need, first of all, to change their social and economic circumstances. We need to rehabilitate them, to improve the quality of their lives, and to bring their economic life to a normal level, so they can provide for themselves and their children.

"When women's standard of living is raised to an adequate level, then we can introduce them to political activities and make them understand what is happening in the world. In their present situation, I don't think they are very keen to know about politics — even about what is happening in our own country."

Margaret Juan's observations apply to many rural women throughout the developing world, not only in Sudan. Survival itself is the daily concern of their lives; what is going on beyond one's village is not a priority. Asked if they had heard of any women leaders in their country or in the world, most rural women were able to name one or two women —usually the wives of male leaders. Few could name any foreign women leaders, with the occasional exception of Queen Elizabeth, Indira Gandhi, or Golda Meir.

In Alexandria, Egypt, an illiterate woman of forty-two who was the mother of nine children told me that she was attending adult literacy classes because she wanted to become educated to "keep up with my children." She hoped that one day she would be able to become a literacy group leader. Conscious of the problems of women in her area, she said that she would have liked to have studied to be a doctor "to help women and teach them about family planning." When I asked her if she could name any women leaders in Egypt or elsewhere, she replied: "I forget them. I guess I don't know any. I really don't bother about things like that. I have so many children and so many responsibilities that I have no time to think about such things."

Another Egyptian woman, in Senoris village in the Fayoum oasis, told me that she had recently learned to read—at age forty—"because then there will be more money." She said she would have liked to have been a nurse or a teacher. When I asked whether she had heard of any women leaders in Egypt, she replied, "Only about Jehan Sadat—I heard about her on the radio."

In all the countries I visited, local officials of women's organizations were the women most often identified by others as leaders. These women quickly become role models for those they serve. Furthermore, the directors of women's organizations often are the *only* leaders to whom rural women have access. Surprisingly, even women with some degree of political consciousness were unaware of women leaders in their countries. A twenty-four-year-old woman I met in a village in central Sri Lanka seemed to have a well-developed awareness of politics, yet she was unable to name women who held high positions in her own country.

"My parents had been in a political organization, and when the time came to organize a women's group in my town, I joined and became a leader. I would like an honest and intelligent husband who has a social conscience and who will join in my activities in social and political affairs. I want a man who is prepared to assume leadership. Women here do not participate enough in public life. They don't have a feeling for the development of the country. That is also because they do not have a good education.

"We need more women representatives because they know the problems of the home, and they are probably better equipped to solve those problems—better than men. I want to be involved in community affairs, to be a good politician, and to do the very best for this village. I want to help my country."

When I asked if she had heard of any women in government service, she replied, "There was a lady who wrote articles on women's activities, but I don't remember her name."

103

Wherever I went in the six countries, it seemed apparent that most women agreed with a Mexican woman—a worker's wife—with whom I talked in a poor suburb of Mexico City. She had had a primary school education and said that she and her husband were saving "to provide a better education for our children." Commenting about the changes that had taken place since her youth, she said: "Women are making progress each day. They have better opportunities now to reach the point men have reached." But upon questioning her further, I found that she was not involved in any activity outside the family. In taking the step from the wish "to be useful" and "to help others" to actual involvement, women are often inhibited by a lack of self-confidence. Maria del Carmen Elu de Lenero, a prominent sociologist, emphasized that women who are accustomed to submissive behavior do not take part in the decision-making process. Their husbands are the ones who decide.

In general, I found that if women were involved in community activities, it was through affiliation with women's organizations (especially in Kenya and Tunisia) or religious groups (in Sri Lanka). The exceptions were women who had had the support and encouragement of their menfolk and who, in most cases, had had the benefit of at least a secondary education. Older women, accustomed to the notion of male supremacy, were inclined to think that only men should enter politics—"because they are stronger." The younger women, however, usually felt that women were equal to men and — given the same educational opportunities — would be as good as men (if not better) as political representatives. These women tended to be educated to some degree and to have some contact with women leaders.

In the small Tunisian village of El Ghrab, I interviewed a forty-year-old woman who told me an unusual story about how she had become interested in advancing the status of women. At age fourteen, she had been married in the traditional manner to a well-to-do village merchant, and now she had seven children. She had not been allowed to attend school as a child, but she said that she could read a bit of Arabic from the Koran. She spent her spare time teaching women in her village about family planning because she realized that "a large family is not a good thing for the mother's health or the family budget."

When I asked whether there was any incident in her life that had particularly influenced her, she told me that she had been taken by her husband to France for the treatment of her asthmatic condition. While watching from her window one afternoon, she had witnessed a women's demonstration in the street. The women were carrying signs and shouting slogans.

"I didn't know what it was all about, but I knew it had to do with women's rights. I saw them and I wanted to join them, but I didn't understand French, so I couldn't do anything. I wanted to join them, to live with them, and participate in their situation.

"Now I want to go to meetings, attend conferences — learn anything about women so that I can teach the women here. I want to meet other women and exchange ideas with them so that we can learn more about each other's lives.

"I want to help our women. I have always wanted to do this, but I find myself in conflict about this with my husband. That's why I would like to be a man, so that I could participate — do what men do. As a woman, I can't do that. It is the lack of education that has left me in this situation."

❧

Fathia Al Assal, the Egyptian playwright, told me that her personal involvement in public life was partly due to her husband's encouragement. She said, however, that when she had become more active outside the home, there came a time when her husband tried to restrict her involvement.

"I give a lot of credit to my husband because he taught me political theory. We women have always had to try to *find* education.

"We were taught to be refined, to be sweet, to be obedient, and to be loving in a world that is difficult. But one week after my marriage, I had a quarrel with my husband. I was not ready to accept his treatment of me as a student—or his building me up as he did all the time. But now I am ready to fight — even with my fists — in political meetings. I know my goals; I don't know the half-way attitude.

"At one point in my marriage, I was beginning to grow independently of my husband. He tried to persuade me to limit my activities and my friendships with men and women, to stay at home and to read. But I stuck to my opinion, arguing that I had to behave first like a free human being, second like a writer, and third like a woman. My husband gave in when I told him that if I didn't begin by being a free woman, then I wouldn't be any good as a writer or as a wife."

❧

Everywhere I spoke with rural women I heard them say that they would like to learn and to help the women around them. I also heard educated women say that they themselves are overextended and lament the lack of women leaders to educate and train the less fortunate women of their countries. Many observed that if the governments were more responsive to women's involvement, perhaps women would venture out more. If a woman's husband is against her participation in the life of the community, a national leader's endorsement of women's involvement may help convince her husband of the need for her contribution.

In Sri Lanka, the sociologist Malsiré Dias commented on her perception of women's political involvement in her country.

"I think there is a tremendous political awareness, but when it comes to participation, that is a little restricted. There are many cultural barriers for women to overcome."

I asked if she saw the same degree of attitudinal change taking place among men as among women.

105

"No, I don't think so. I think there are very few men who have actually changed from their past behavior. There is still some preference shown to the boy children, the males. That is part of our tradition. Not in the school system, but within the family, where the parents feel a greater responsibility toward preparing the males for future life—especially for employment. As you know, there is always the cultural preference for men — boy children. I don't think the men are anti-women. It has just been a tradition, and women are not able to break through. Gradually they are succeeding in getting certain jobs that have always been reserved for men."

Dorothy Abeywickreme and Kumari Jayawardene each shared a positive perception of women's roles in political participation and leadership in Sri Lanka. Dorothy Abeywickreme, president of the Association of University Women, told me that she believes that the increasing involvement of young women in public life is one of the major changes taking place in Sri Lankan society:

"The one principal change in recent years is the political change. Middle-class women are now more politically minded, more politically active. In the past, women didn't take part in political activity. They would shy away from that kind of thing. But despite the progress, I think we still need to educate women for political activities. That is how their horizons are widened."

Kumari Jayawardene saw sharp differences in awareness of social issues along generational lines:

"Now we are finding that there is a new group of young leaders coming up. For example, I don't have to traipse around the country so much on the women's issues anymore." Smiling, she added, "And the twenty-five-year-old men are far more liberal than their fathers."

The less-educated or illiterate women expressed a different opinion about women's involvement outside the family. An elderly, poor, and illiterate woman I interviewed in Kenya represented the views of the older women in all of the countries I visited. From the vantage point of her seventy years, she did not have much faith in the capabilities of women. I asked her whether she thought boys and girls should have the same education.

"My feeling is that a boy should be more educated than a girl. I believe that a man is more clever than a woman. The brain of a man is bigger. Whether a woman is educated or not, she cannot be equal to a man. A woman's brain is not the same."

Was there ever a time, I asked, when she had said to herself that it would have been better to have been born a man? "I have never thought that," she said. "I am happy to be a woman." But why not a man, I suggested, since she had said men's brains were better. She replied that she had never wished to be a man: "It is *other* people who say men have good brains. But I think in jobs and outside the family, men can work better than women. In the home, women are better than men."

Most of the younger women I encountered in Kenya and in the other countries had shed such ambiguous feelings about the equality of men and women. The views of an eighteen-year-old woman in Kisumu, Kenya, were representative of those of the younger generation elsewhere. The young woman was attending an adult literacy class. She said she believed that men and women were equal but that women leaders would better understand the needs of women. When I asked her how she would vote if a man and a woman with the same education and qualifications were running against one another for a seat in parliament, she replied:

"I would vote for the woman, because if a woman has a political post, she will say to those who elected her, 'This is my friend. Let me help her.' A man will just pass by them and say, 'I don't know this woman.' It is important for women to be involved in the community and in government."

In Nyeri, Kenya, another young woman told me, "I would even vote for a woman for president of the republic." And in Mombasa, at a group meeting, a woman commented:

"I think the men hate the idea that a woman can speak up—the idea that a woman can voice her views. But I hope that one day we are going to be able to get our way. I know we'll do it—slowly. I think women could really run the country much better than men because men are very selfish. They just think about themselves; they don't think about others."

Another participant in the Mombasa discussion added:

"Women are now starting to fight for their rights and to enter parliament and local councils. They are defeating men. And when, after the elections, men realize that women have really won, they get that hatred in their hearts. They don't like to be governed by women. Africans *especially* don't like it."

Yet many women remain apprehensive about, or even fear, taking up a role in public life. Uninformed about their legal rights, encumbered by timidity and traditional notions of a "woman's place," or fearful of ridicule and insults, they continue to stay out of politics. A villager in Kenya told me, "Politics is not for women. You have to take insults and bad language. You have to be very strong." Even Jehan Sadat, the wife of President Anwar Sadat of Egypt, told me how uncomfortable she had felt at the outset of her public career.

"I used to work even before my husband was President," she told me. "When I started the Telah Society for raising the living standards of peasants, I used to organize meetings for both men and women. The women sat on one side and the men on the other. I didn't sit in front of them, as I do now. On the contrary, I used to sit beside the women, not up front, facing all the people.

"We explained what we wanted to do for the people there and how we wanted to raise the standard of living of women so they could help the men. I told them it was for their good, for the sake of the family.

"By the third year, I was sitting in *front* of them, but at the beginning it was difficult — facing the men of the village. I was certain their mentality would lead them to say: 'Who is this woman? She is very forward, she is like men; she is not a woman.' And they would not have paid attention to me. It is better to take everything gradually, step by step."

Near Kisumu, Kenya, I talked with a twenty-three-year-old mother who was attending training to become a teacher at the Kenyatta Institute. She said she believed women were "advancing," but she felt that men were superior. She voiced an opinion I heard often: women *should* be involved, "but it is not for me." I asked her what she thought about the role of women in politics.

"My opinion is that in the past we have been considered just mothers who should be staying home in the kitchen. But because of social change —everything is changing—we ought to do *everything*. We must contribute so that we make sure our country will improve in the future. In my opinion, I say that even women can do it."

I asked her whether she would personally like to get involved in local politics.

"As for me, I don't like it. I would rather do something else. I don't have a good reason, but I'm sure I wouldn't like it. Politics takes someone who is courageous and who can stand up and be insulted. You can't say you mind abusive words. And then, coming home late, sometimes it is too risky for your life. I would prefer to do something other than politics."

The risks faced by a woman entering the national political arena can be grave. During my interview with Julia Ojiambo, I asked her to talk about her campaign for parliament—having heard she had been the object of bitter opposition because she was a woman.

"At first I was discriminated against. They said, 'A woman? It must be a joke.' Then we started campaigning, and they changed quickly — because of what 'the woman' was able to do. When we started talking about politics, they noticed more the ability and knowledge, and listened to what was said. That was the end of their prejudice, except for the five men who were fighting against me. They were the only ones who had all the nasty things to say about the woman candidate. Since those against me were from the same tribe, I believe they did it to me only because I am a woman; they didn't do it to the other candidates—the men.

"It was one of the worst, toughest campaigns in Kenya. When the men realized I was gaining on them, they were frightened. They threatened lightly at first, and then more. They threatened to beat up my family, to destroy our home, and they did all sorts of things to frighten us. They beat up my relatives so that I would give up. The last day, they nearly killed my husband. He has a big scar—they slashed the top of his head. They beat up one of my cousins. He is maimed permanently—they cut into his head. Very many of my people were injured. That was to frighten us so that we would give up. But my family just said, 'If it means dying, we will die.' "

I asked Julia Ojiambo if she thought these events frighten other women from public office, or if she felt she had shown that a breakthrough was possible.

"Oh, it has given women wonderful encouragement. Now they want to do it the way I did it. They will *fight* to get in. They don't want it any other way. They don't want it said, 'You got in easily because you are a woman.' No one said that to me. All the members of parliament *know* I got elected in a very difficult way. None of them had such difficulties."

The story of the Ojiambo campaign was well known throughout Kenya. To some it had given heart, to others it had brought fear.

❧

A Kenyan woman I met in Busia was convinced that women, too, had political obligations. Illiterate herself, she hoped that her children would be able to attend school as long as possible. She had been abandoned by her husband thirteen years earlier and had joined a women's agricultural cooperative, enabling her to earn the money necessary for her children's school fees. When I asked her whether there was any law that protected women from abandonment by their husbands, she replied:

"I am not aware of the protection of the law, but I would like the government to do more. Here only the men run for election. The women don't. Now there is a woman—Julia Ojiambo. I voted for her. We're waiting to see if there's another woman who will run. I hope that in the next parliament there will be only women."

❧

The importance of leadership training—and of the existence of women's organizations to provide it—was emphasized constantly by women leaders. In Egypt, Jehan Sadat told me:

"We need women's organizations to go to the villages and speak with women. If men are sent, it is completely impossible for them to contact women. Through other women, of course, it is much easier."

But as I heard over and over again in the six countries, women leaders are not numerous. In Juba, Sudan, Margaret Juan reported this need for trained women:

"Most of our women leaders here in Sudan are not as yet well-versed in Sudanese politics or in the politics of socialism. We need proper education and orientation from women leaders—seminars and lectures given by women from Khartoum. It is important to develop women's confidence.

"Those who really understand the process of politics are very few. There are women who may be active in their work or in other things. They may be intellectuals, but they don't understand politics. There are others who may not be educated but who, through experience, have learned a lot of things. It is through this second group of women that we can communicate our message because, you see, the participation of uneducated women is *vital* if we are to help women move up and get proper training.

"If women who are confined to their homes see women in other countries coming up to challenge the men—to talk bluntly about women and about what women should do to liberate themselves, what they should do to contribute to the economic, social, and political development of their country—I think they will be encouraged to do the same. Change will eventually come, but it is going to take a long time."

A colleague of Margaret Juan's, a social worker at the Ministry of Social Welfare in Port Sudan, commented on another aspect of the involvement of women in Sudanese public life:

"Sudanese women are frightened to talk about politics or law. I don't know why. I can't tell you if it is their lack of education or fear of their husbands or fathers or what. I think it is very important to know the leaders. Even in discussions between you and your husband, you must learn and know something about the leaders of your country.

"The basic need of women is education. We have fewer schools for girls than for boys. In this area, for example, there are only two secondary schools for girls but six for boys. I think education will help everything else. And it is the responsibility of women who are qualified to educate other women—to go out to the rural areas to show women how to manage their lives, as well as to show them how to be healthy, how to bring up their children, and how to do manual work and any work that can help them. We are trying to do that."

The social worker pointed out that many Sudanese women fear male disapproval if they participate in public life. Her opinion was supported when, the next day, we visited El Husheri, a village south of Port Sudan. The solitary schoolmaster of the dusty wooden school, which was attended by children of nomadic tribes, complained bitterly that his village received little attention or help from the authorities. Malnutrition and disease were such serious problems in the village that they had in fact become his main preoccupation. When I asked him if members of the women's organization came to aid women of the settlement, he replied:

"The Sudanese Women's Union concentrates on towns only. The women don't go out because of their husbands and transportation difficulties. But even if transportation were available, they still wouldn't go out because of custom."

I asked what he thought of this situation. He shrugged his shoulders, shook his head in a resigned way, and said, "Customs and traditions are at fault—men's customs."

When there are relatively few educated women able or willing to undertake it, the task of helping rural women is at best an enormous one. The few women who are educated and active have difficulty in keeping up with the demands placed upon them in their professional lives, in their voluntary activities for the advancement of women, and within their families.

Fathia M'Zali, president of the National Union of Tunisian Women, is a woman who faces such multiple demands daily. She has been active in politics since her student days, when she participated in the movement for Tunisia's independence from France. Today, as president of an organization that initiates and directs programs designed to educate and involve women in nation-building, she has difficulty finding women who are willing to take on organizational responsibilities:

"At one point, there was a lot of criticism leveled against educated women who didn't contribute to public life — who didn't serve. But a woman who is an intellectual begins with many years of studying. Then she has a profession, responsibilities. But she may also have a home and children. And if the children are young, can she really do anything else but take care of her family?

"We now see a growth in women's participation, but personally, I get the impression that women who work — and there are many who work now—are *tired*. They don't have much time to do other things. The number of working women is growing—simply because the number of educated women is growing. But I don't know if the balance can be found.

"For example, we have now proposed to the National Assembly—I am a member of the Assembly—that we establish a minimum percentage of women candidates for the municipal elections. I wanted women to hold at least a minimum percentage of seats. I wanted to force men to make room for women. But there was opposition to this. People said, 'Why do you want to *limit* the number of women when, in fact, they are equal? They can have 50 per cent of the seats, and if you accept 20 per cent, you limit them.'

"As for me, when I was asked whether I would like to be head of a municipality, I said, 'No, enough is enough! Others will have to do it. I have enough activities as it is.'"

Fathia M'Zali's story typifies the situation of many women activists. Now forty-nine, the mother of six children, and wife of the Minister of Health, she has experienced difficulties that are familiar to women who have attempted to serve their country in full-time, high-level positions.

"In Tunisia, I think I am considered a bit of an exception," she said, "My parents and my children feel this when they compare me to other mothers. My husband is very active; so am I. My children objected when I accepted the position of president of the Women's Union. They had had enough. They thought we were both too politically minded, too active. My children would like to keep me as a mother. When I read the newspaper at the table they say, 'That's the end. We've had it. You have become just like our father.'"

Self-confidence, awareness of legal rights, the training of women leaders, and the acceptance by men of women's participation were all repeatedly cited as essential to expanding women's involvement in public life. It was widely assumed, however, that bringing about these changes "will take much time."

This suggested that women in the developing countries — like women in developed countries—underestimate their potential political power. As Julia Ojiambo, for one, pointed out:

"The women in Kenya *are* the voters. They have the biggest vote. They could literally control the election if they wished. They participate in all the campaigns, rallies, and meetings. When it actually comes down to the polling date, they'll be there. The men will probably say, 'I'll come later.' But the women will always vote."

During my visit to an Indian village in southern Mexico, women's involvement in public office received an unexpected endorsement. As the women of the family were discussing local affairs in a peasant home in San Sebastien, the husband of one of the women entered the house. He listened for a while and then suddenly interrupted, saying:

"The reason men don't want to have women in authority is because they don't want women giving them orders. They are accustomed to giving orders themselves, and they don't want women doing it. That's very clear. But I wish a woman would get elected mayor of this town. The men haven't done any good. All they do is get drunk. We should give women a chance to see if they can do better."

# 8

AFTERWORD

# "Come learn,
but go to the people,
and listen"

AFTERWORD

The words of Victoria Yar Arol quoted in the title of this chapter constitute a plea for much closer attention to the human dimension in development. The interviews recorded in this volume show that women — when listened to — articulate attitudes, beliefs, and aspirations that could constructively influence the development process. And as we shall see in this last chapter, they make concrete suggestions which planners should consider.

What surprised and moved me most as I listened to women in such very different cultural settings was the striking commonality — whether they were educated or illiterate, urban or rural — of their most basic values: the importance they assign to family, dignity, and service to others. Their replies to questions about self-advancement opportunities showed — recalling the words of E.F. Schumacher — that they seek "to *be* more, not to *have* more." They want more contemporary roles, to be sure, but roles that draw their strength from the collaborative traditions of the past. They say that they seek solidarity between men and women in improving the well-being of their families and communities. What many fear, however, is that the rapid changes brought by "development" are weakening family relationships and thus even the family itself.

As rural women enumerated the changes taking place in the community around them — as they questioned me about the world beyond the village — they spoke of their frustrations and their feelings of inadequacy. They repeatedly stated that the change from a subsistence economy to a money economy had resulted in stress within the family. Western modes of development — tending to emphasize urban growth and male employment — have increased disparities between men and women in all areas of life: physical and social mobility, economic and political status, and interpersonal relationships. Usually one member of the couple, the man, is a participant in the cash economy — if he can find work; the other, the woman, remains dependent upon traditional tasks, since she has neither the skills nor the personal mobility to permit her to participate in the changing economy. To add to this scenario of increasing disparities, the woman finds that the value of her traditional role is diminished by the new emphasis on *paid* work. She no longer feels as

115

respected or as useful as she once was. These factors, together with the rising cost of living, have made women realize that they cannot, as one Tunisian woman said, just "remain *there*—where life put us." They want to learn and participate in their community's advancement. Yet barriers of custom and tradition and the absence of learning opportunities continue to bind millions of women to submissive, nonparticipatory roles.

It is true, of course, that men also encounter problems in adapting to rapid change in "developing" societies. Migration, unemployment, the loneliness of the migrant wage earner, the anonymity of urban life, and the growing difficulty of communicating with family members who have not shared these experiences are factors that contribute to their disorientation. Nevertheless, it is the women who are hit hardest by these changes. As village women told me: "Men are moving ahead." "Men and women are growing apart." "Men look down on us—I don't know why." "There is not as much trust between men and women as before." "Sons don't take care of their mothers anymore; they just go off elsewhere and forget us." In both urban and rural areas, the uneducated women with whom I spoke fear the changing ways of men, which they believe result in men's disregard of women's worth.

Despite the variety of their cultural settings, the women I interviewed expressed similar, simple perceptions of a "good life" and of personal dignity: they want healthy, educated children; respect for their efforts to serve and raise the family; and the understanding and encouragement of their husbands. They want a chance to learn, to participate, to "keep up with the times," to help others—to improve their lives and the lives of those around them. "We want to develop," they say, "but men and women *together*." The importance that many of the more self-assured women—both rural and urban—attributed to the influence of supportive fathers and husbands on their lives and achievements suggests the positive effects men can have on the advancement of women.

In most cases, however, women's desire to adapt to the changing times precedes the evolution of customs that govern their lives, creating conflicts with those who would restrain them to outmoded roles. Many women suggested that traditional male dominance — the idea of male superiority — was the most disabling custom of all. Restricted mobility, inferior legal status, arranged marriages, and economic dependence are but a few of the male-dominance-related factors that tie women to submissive behavior and to feelings of inferiority. To overcome their fears and to participate in society as they wish, women must be assured of basic legal rights; they must have access to better health care and nutrition assistance, and to literacy and skill training; and they must have the opportunity to gain more autonomy and self-confidence. As many women leaders acknowledged, to break out of their isolation and to become involved as partners in the development of their societies, women must obtain a sense of their own self-worth and potential. "But first the laws must be changed," the same leaders emphasized.

In several of the nations I visited, the legal equality of men and women remains unfinished business. Laws governing the status of women are varied, poorly enforced, and frequently ignored. If women live in a world of male dominance and lack legal protection or knowledge of the law, how can they contribute to the development of their societies? How, for example, can a woman attend a literacy class if she is not allowed out of her home? How can she hope to make the family land more productive when she has no access to credit? In some countries, reform of family law — setting a minimum marriage age, requiring consent to marriage by both members of a couple, protecting the child regardless of its birth in or out of wedlock, assuring women of protection from inequitable divorce or abandonment, granting rights to foreign-born wives, and recognizing women's title to family property — are a necessary basis for the improvement of the status of women as well as for their participation in activities outside the home.

Health and nutrition conditions among the disadvantaged majority of the population in many developing nations remain inadequate, and— as doctors in several of the countries I visited told me — the health of women, especially in the rural areas, often is inferior to that of men in the same family. Reasons for this disparity include the system of food distribution within the family and the physical demands of chores, coupled with frequent pregnancies and the lengthy nursing of infants. Many women say that they themselves want small families, but that their resort to family planning services depends on the consent of their husbands, who often still cling to the traditional norm of wanting "as many children as come."

Population program planners have not yet fully understood that few women dare make the decision *on their own* to control family size by the use of contraceptives. To make matters worse, many family planning programs continue to preach about "family responsibility" to women only, thereby confronting the couple with another source of discord. If women are to be enabled to plan the spacing of their children—indeed, if the population growth rate is to be significantly lowered — then husbands, too, must be the target of family planning programs. Time and again I was asked, "Would you please speak to my husband? He won't listen. He wants more children, and I'm so tired."

Another suggestion made by the women interviewed was the provision of sex education in schools. The importance of "preparation for responsible parenthood" — for *both* boys and girls — was repeatedly emphasized by mothers, social workers, and family planning personnel. The timidity that inhibits members of a couple from discussing sex with one another is also present in their relationships with children; and it is usually the young girls who suffer the consequences of this silence.

The major need of the women interviewed is clearly *practical* education and training. They believe that an opportunity to learn health and nutrition skills will benefit their families—that if they learn a marketable skill, they will contribute to the family's income, and thereby to the improvement of its health, nutrition, and general well-being.

Few policymakers fully understand the extent of the responsibilities carried by rural women in developing societies. Recognition of women's need to acquire income-generating skills will require attitudinal changes on the part of those policymakers. The rural women with whom I spoke do not seek "busywork"; they seek survival for their families. Planners should also assure that the training offered to women does not relegate them to underpaid, low-status employment, and that the skills taught relate to local needs and markets. Agricultural techniques, marketing and budgeting, simple mechanics, animal husbandry, water management, and public health are only a few examples of simple skills that can be learned and passed on to others easily. Moreover, as many observers now emphasize, if the plans and programs designed to increase women's participation in development are going to get the desired response, then women themselves must also participate in their formation and in their execution.

In all six nations, illiterate mothers echoed the words of a Sri Lankan woman who told me: "For us it is too late, but our children must learn to cope with this life. They must get an education." At the same time, women leaders often stressed the *changing* educational needs of youth in developing nations. Colonial education systems are outmoded, and new systems, based on the needs of the country and its people, are required. In Egypt, for example, Zahia Marzouk said: "We must understand the situation of the younger people and try to help them. They are not living in the same conditions as we did. We have to understand the changes that are taking place." She also voiced her concern for nonsexist education: "Enlightened education would eliminate notions of the superiority of one sex or another"—notions which ultimately influence the structure of the family and society.

Teacher training is a priority need if educational systems are to keep up with the demand for schooling, which is increasing rapidly, primarily due to population growth. Fathia M'Zali, president of the National Union of Tunisian Women, pointed out that in many developing nations there is a lack of competent, trained adults to teach youngsters. "Parents just can't cope, and youth organizations don't have enough personnel to guide the youngsters. The evolution here has been too rapid. Everything has changed so quickly — and the youngsters are too numerous in proportion to the adults trained to work with them." In villages in Sudan, Sri Lanka, and Mexico, I was told that there simply are not enough teachers to serve the rural areas: "The teacher only comes once in a while. Some days yes, some days no." Special incentives need to be offered if more teachers are to be attracted to remote areas.

In the six countries visited, women have the right to vote, yet their replies to questions concerning public affairs revealed a lack of interest in political issues and a lack of knowledge about their political representatives. Several women leaders said that they believe women's hesitancy to participate in public issues to be due to their centuries-old sense of inferiority. Women themselves are generally unaware of their political clout, although politicians often appeal to them for their vote. Women have been told ad infinitum to "keep quiet and mind the kitchen." Venturing out in public, speaking one's opinion—or, in some cases, even *having* an opinion—often demand great personal courage. The importance of women's organizations in helping women to overcome timidity and lack of self-confidence was stressed time and again. With the assistance of effective women's organizations or community development groups, more women will begin to participate from the outset in designing and implementing the projects that affect them.

Women leaders wisely suggested considering the needs of rural women in both short- and long-term perspectives. *Short-term* needs, I was told, demand, first and foremost, personal self-confidence and an understanding of women's importance in community and national life. Then, to aid them in their tasks within the family, women need practical instruction in health, nutrition, family planning, and in earning skills. Leadership training and education for rural girls were pointed out by both leaders and rural women as a major priority. To become involved as *participants* in the community, they need contact with other women, civic education, and knowledge of legislation and rights.

*Long-term* needs, they said, include research on the changing situation, roles, and requirements of women at the local, regional, and national levels. To coordinate such research, a legitimate national agency, authorized to study, develop, and implement policy, and having the budget and power to do so, is necessary. Repeatedly I heard women leaders lament the fact that so little is known about the needs of rural women — and, consequently, about the means of aiding rural families.

A variety of specific program suggestions also emerged in the course of my four months of interviews with the women whose words are the basis of this book. These suggestions are itemized here not because they are new — although some of them may be — but because it is important for planners to know that they were articulated either by poor rural and urban women themselves, or by women leaders who make a point of staying close to the "grass roots."

1. Far more emphasis on training *women* field workers — paramedics, midwives, nutrition field workers, and family planning workers — could bring health services to a greater number of rural families. Some women do not have the "right" to travel to a health clinic; others have husbands who forbid them to be treated by a male doctor; for still others, "it is too far to the nearest clinic." Male field workers are not easily accepted in homes, and, if admitted, often find it difficult to set the more timid women at ease. As Jehan Sadat has stressed: "We need *women* to reach the rural woman. Men just can't have contact with our women."

2. Whether they are funded by international or by bilateral agencies, many training programs — as well as meetings of labor unionists, medical personnel, population experts, teachers, etc. — still fail to involve women or to benefit from their participation. Sensitizing professionals to the advancement of women starts with their training, and *women trainers* as well as *women trainees* will make that training effective.

3. The involvement of more *women rural development officers* could increase the adoption of labor-saving techniques by women. In some countries, new techniques and resources simply are not accessible to rural women because only male teachers are available to instruct in the use of such techniques — and the custom of female seclusion prevents women from attending classes taught and attended by men.

4. *Those who (already) have served in remote areas should receive special consideration as priority candidates for further training.* Whether they are

rural development officers, teachers, or paramedical personnel, those who have served (and served well) in rural areas should be rewarded with training opportunities that contribute to the advancement of their careers. This might provide an incentive for capable young people who are reluctant to spend one or two years far from urban centers.

5. *Support for self-help and volunteer efforts* should be a priority concern of aid agencies which should provide both technical and financial assistance. I visited a building in Port Sudan that had been set aside as "a meeting and learning place" for the poorer women of the neighborhood. It was hoped that the women would be taught sewing, cooking, and handicrafts at the same time that they were instructed in family planning and child care. For several months the women had continued to come, but no courses were ever offered. There was a sewing machine, but no one knew how to operate it. Women were willing to bring their food to learn new methods of cooking, but there were no pots and pans, and no money for kerosene for the demonstration stove. With adequate equipment, one trained woman could have taught skills to provide clothing, a source of income, and improved nutrition to all who chose to come. No such person was available for the task. If prestige and recognition were associated with volunteer service, perhaps candidates would be more numerous. The story of Miss Janet, the physically handicapped leader of the M'Bale women's group in Kenya, is a demonstration of such skill transfer and how it has improved the health and nutrition of some fifty families.

6. Simple grist mills, improved water sources nearer villages, hand pumps, etc., are some obvious examples of *simple technologies* (and time-saving devices) that could aid rural women. In Egypt, I met an official who was experimenting with small mobile solar ovens that were strikingly similar in appearance to modern baby strollers. We ate corn, barley, and chicken cooked in this invention. If perfected and adopted (and if not too costly), such a "solar cooker" would save women many hours that now are spent scavenging for wood (and perhaps even slow down the process of deforestation in some areas). However, the manner of introducing technology at the village level must be very carefully considered. As Dr. Marilyn Carr, among others, has cautioned: "The modern equipment which has been introduced has inevitably been aimed at men and has often resulted in more, rather than less, work for women. For example, partial mechanization can all too often help men clear more land with less effort while the women are left to weed and harvest a greater acreage with traditional implements."* Some cultural barriers also hinder the adoption of labor-saving techniques. A woman social worker in Kenya told me of her reluctance to suggest the idea of using idle family cattle to carry firewood and water; she said she was already the subject of jokes among her male colleagues because she was attempting to introduce new techniques for performing traditional chores. Yet, as she pointed out, rural families could greatly benefit from the adoption of this idea.

---

*Populi (*journal of the U.N. Fund for Population Activities*), Vol. 3, No. 4, 1976, p. 48.

7. *Low-cost credit should be made available to women's self-help groups and cooperatives.* I visited cooperative day-care centers, stores, and housing projects started by women's groups with the aid of small loans. In other places, I was told that credit was refused to women unless they were landowners or were accompanied by a man when they came to apply.

8. Several women told me of their experiences with village cooperatives that were managed by men. When women brought in the crops that they themselves had planted and harvested, the earnings were automatically turned over to their husbands. Many echoed the words of a woman in Kenya who said that the earnings from her crop were spent "in the bars—instead of on school fees for the children." Some women said they were not allowed to participate in a cooperative because they were not landowners. Some also voiced complaints about the marketing of handicrafts (pottery, rugs, baskets, etc.). Often only the men have the mobility (or time) to leave the village to sell crafts elsewhere. Women were paid only small sums for their crafts, although the men made big profits at market. They suggested *women's cooperatives* for marketing farm produce and handicrafts. But women need access to credit, they say, and knowledge of accounting and sales techniques.

9. Home industries and crafts have become a subject of debate among development policymakers and practitioners. Some planners argue that women should be taught more advanced, nontraditional skills —and not crafts, which relegate them to traditional roles. It is true that handicraft markets often have only limited possibilities and that the returns on labor invested tend to be too low. On the basis of my conversations with women leaders and with rural women themselves, however, I am not convinced that this argument necessarily is in the best interest of families that urgently need assistance. If handicrafts provide immediate earnings—cash in hand with which to feed the family *this* week—why should a woman be told that handicrafts hinder her advancement? If her family needs the income *now*, in order to survive, she may not be able to take the time to learn a more sophisticated skill—even if she has access to programs that can provide it. *Integrated programs that teach crafts simultaneously with more advanced skills*—to be used at a later date—may be the solution. Fathia M'Zali, president of the Tunisian National Women's Union, told me of a program that taught bookbinding to illiterate rural girls, in addition to the traditional embroidery and sewing classes. She said that the fact that bookbinding could be practiced inside as well as outside the home made the course very popular; girls who were not allowed to work outside the home could utilize this training to earn cash.

10. I was told that modern, Western-style housing does not in most cases serve traditional family communication patterns. In Tunisia and Egypt the government has recognized this problem and has begun the construction of homes whose design takes into account the roles of all family members, old and young. These "new traditional" homes provide for the needs of animals, the storage of crops, and child care. I was told that *the involvement of women in the design of housing projects* might help to alleviate problems of alienation and anxiety that are at present intensified in most urban housing programs.

The implementation of suggestions such as these could benefit immeasurably from the involvement of women's organizations and the communciations media — two major resources that were present but vastly underutilized in several of the countries I visited.

In communities where women are bound by strict traditions, *the involvement of women's organizations,* which remain largely ignored by development planners, is essential to women's advancement. In most male-oriented cultures, women receive information primarily from other women; thus the "women's network" is the most practical one through which to reach women. Another benefit of such organizations is the contact they foster among women, which develops self-confidence. If women's organizations — often distinguished by their good will and lack of funds—had more access to leadership training and funding, they could be more effective in offering training in income-earning skills, literacy, health care, and family planning counseling.

To become effective change agents, however, women's groups will need the support — both financial and moral — of national leadership. Financial support is needed to provide vehicles, gasoline, teaching tools, and training programs. Also, a staff of trained — and paid — leaders would be a positive step in strengthening organizational structures. Those who have been relegated to the usually unrecognized role of volunteer program director would gain in status and public credibility if given even a small stipend.

The moral support of women's organizations by national leaders is equally important. In societies where women have just begun to participate in community affairs, a husband's (or neighbor's) mockery can stifle a woman's will to serve. When service is associated with prestige because it is recognized by national leaders, resistance is minimized. It should be noted, however, that in some nations, women's organizations are closely tied to the dominant political party, and funding made available to them thus might be subject to political pressure or used in ways other than what the women's organizations would prefer. To avoid such political pressure situations, development agencies could provide grants for specific projects. In cases where the government prohibits direct aid, nongovernmental organizations might serve as a channel for project funds.

The *communications media* still are rarely utilized, I found, in systematic efforts to reach rural women with practical information. Many of the women with whom I spoke criticized the radio for its lack of educational programs. They mentioned the need for "family life programs" to provide information on hygiene, health, child care, and nutrition. At the same time, many said their preferred programs were news, music, and soap operas — all of which could be oriented to learning practical skills. Zahia Marzouk of Alexandria has written songs about family responsibility and family planning that were at first sung only at wedding festivities. They have become popular, however, and are now also sung elsewhere; the music and the words carry the message.

Another example of learning through music was a song sung to me by the women of a cooperative farm in northwestern Kenya. The village had been the scene of a cholera epidemic the year before; nearly one third of the village had died. Following a group discussion, as I was about to leave, the women insisted on singing a song that they themselves had composed. It was loud, rhythmic, and joyous. When I asked about its subject, the interpreter explained it was the story of the cholera epidemic, of the deaths that had ensued, and of how to keep the "witch cholera" out of the house and village in the future. These village women had created a musical learning tool that could be passed on to others via the radio.

In most developing nations, radio and television are owned and operated by the government. A ministry of information or culture decides all program content. Some nations have made good use of the media as a learning tool; others have ignored its potential for educational purposes and have often resorted instead to imported foreign programming (which I heard criticized repeatedly). Intelligent radio programming could, for example, help eradicate demeaning superstitions, make suggestions for village improvement projects, deliver information on public health, and teach civic responsibility to citizens — providing education at a low cost to a large segment of the population.

The involvement of the media and of the women's organizations in the development effort depends largely upon the support of government agencies — and thus the role of national leadership is crucial. A commitment at the highest level is necessary to involve women in national planning, to unequivocally support women's efforts to help themselves, and to use the media to its fullest potential for the education of rural families.

Development agencies, government planners, international public servants, and chiefs of state—if indeed they wish to serve as positive change agents—need to become far more sensitive to the roles and involvement of women in development efforts and need to include women in decision making at all levels. Unfortunately, this is not often the case. Several officials I met even ridiculed the entire "women in development" concept. One international development official simply could not understand why I wanted to travel around the countryside in order to, as he put it, "talk to all those ignorant women." Yet the man's position was one of enormous influence on the development policies of the nation in which he was stationed. Fortunately, I also met male officials who were sympathetic to my assignment. One doctor even asked me to "go home and write about the situation of women here. If we don't get pressure from abroad—from the outside—no one here will pay attention to their problems."

In her small office in the outskirts of Nairobi, Pheobe Aseyio, director of the Child Welfare Association of Kenya, pointed out another attitudinal problem common to development assistance efforts:

123

"You have the experts who come and point down, saying, 'This is the way you must do it,' basing their argument on what they have seen elsewhere. They don't take the time — and we need much more time than the developed peoples—to let ideas emerge from the grass roots. If you are patient enough to take the time for ideas to emerge, maybe we can strike the balance."

We are now well advanced into the U.N. Decade for Women (1976-1985). While it remains difficult to obtain information about what is actually being planned in countries throughout the world, it certainly is possible to monitor United Nations programs for women and rural development, to exchange information with Third World women leaders, and to make a serious attempt to reinforce the international network among women. Without exception, the women with who I spoke — whether they were well-educated or illiterate — were curious about women in other nations. They wanted to exchange ideas with them, and, as they said, "to learn from one another." Victoria Yar Arol has offered wise words of warning to guide such exchanges. "Yes, we would welcome the interest and help of women from abroad — it is important that women understand each other and work together, " she said. "But first they must be willing to listen. Not *tell. Listen.*"

"Rural women want to speak for themselves," Kathryn F. Clarenbach has written, "and to have their voices solicited and listened to; they want to be recognized as significant and contributing members of their families and of society at large; they want to have the opportunity to become independent persons, to control their own lives, to have a role in the formulation of public policy and to share somewhat equitably in the fruits of our society."* This statement, included in a report of the National Advisory Council on Women's Educational Programs, applies to American rural women. But the same words describe the aspirations of the rural women with whom I spoke in the six nations visited — attesting to the commonality of the most fundamental human needs and aspirations of women (and men) in all nations.

The integration of women in world development programs is a complex undertaking. It involves attitudinal change, institutional change, legislative measures, and the eradication of customs that bind women to outmoded beliefs and roles. Development planners, international public servants, and program officers in developing countries should begin to search for solutions in the very places where they must be made to work — in the villages of developing regions. If not, development will con-

---

*Educational Needs of Rural Women and Girls: Report of the National Advisory Council on Women's Educational Programs (*Washington, D.C.: U.S. Government Printing Office, January 1977*), p. 12.*

tinue to be a haphazard affair suffering from irrelevant and elitist views of the needs of the world's poorest people. I believe that the words of the women who speak out in this book prove that those who have been voiceless far too long have much to contribute — to national development and to our common future. But first they must be given the opportunity to do so.

ANNEX A

BEHIND THE SCENES:
A CONTENT ANALYSIS OF THE INTERVIEWS

Annex A

# Behind the Scenes:
# A Content Analysis of the Interviews

Mayra Buvinić with
Pandora Anwyl, Luann Martin, and Jennefer Sebstad

Perdita Huston's interviews convey personalized portraits of the lives, thoughts, and feelings of women in six Third World countries. The descriptive detail generated by the actual taped interviews can also be used to learn more about what the women conveyed in sum. At the request of Perdita Huston and of the U.S. Agency for International Development, the authors undertook a systematic analysis of the transcripts of 123 of Huston's interviews to find out what predominant themes and concerns the women expressed. The findings of this analysis complement Huston's selective recollections by going "behind the scenes" and focusing on the "composite message," emphasizing both what the women actually said and what they more indirectly revealed about their priorities and needs.

In interviewing women in six countries, Huston followed an unstructured format: she let the women speak for themselves. Because the number of women interviewed was comparatively small, the findings described here are subject to two major limitations: 1) they cannot be generalized to women other than those who conversed with Huston, and 2) they may mask subtle cultural and behavioral differences among the women.

If the inability to generalize the results is the main drawback of this method, the information produced has a major advantage over usual social science data; the question and answer format of standard questionnaires and survey methodologies restricts the interviewee's range of responses and predetermines the topics that the interviewee addresses. Especially when the social scientist is not familar with the problem, the people, or the particular situation, this format tends to cloud important dimensions of the issue being investigated. While *unstructured* interviews like the ones Huston conducted are never free of biases (since the interviewer's personal characteristics as well as situational factors inevitably influence the types of responses given), such interviews are less subject than structured ones to biases arising from the interviewer's choice of topics or from his/her control over the responses given by the interviewee. Unstructured interviews have the advantage of providing respondents with the chance to shape the content of the conversation. A major result of this content analysis of Huston's interviews is a rank ordering of the themes the women brought up in their conversations. From this ranking, the importance that the women themselves give to some issues over others in their lives can be inferred.

*This interview content analysis was conducted at the International Center for Research on Women, Washington, D.C. It was supported by the Office of Women in Development of the U.S. Agency for International Development. The views expressed herein are those of the authors and do not necessarily represent those of either the ICRW or of AID.*

## METHOD OF ANALYSIS

This content analysis is based on transcripts of individual interviews with 123 women. Fifty-four (54) per cent of these women are from rural areas and 46 per cent from urban areas; 60 per cent are literate and 40 per cent are illiterate.[1] Thirty-one (31) per cent of the women are from Kenya; the other five countries are represented in the population interviewed in proportions varying from 11 per cent to 17 per cent. (See Table 1.) Although the findings cannot be generalized (for the reasons noted above) to women other than the 123 in the sample, they should prove useful in generating hypotheses for future testing using scientific field methods. The women's responses reflect their needs and attitudes, perceptions and opinions, but do not necessarily reflect objective conditions or what women actually do (or would do) in a specific situation. The responses represent conditions as perceived by the women or as the women wanted the interviewer to perceive them.[2]

A modified version of the standard content analysis method was used to analyze the data. The standard method first defines the categories and sub-categories and then classifies the data; i.e., the process is one of going from categorization to analysis. In this exercise, the process was of necessity different. Because we were not familiar with the material, we had to alternate between examining the interviews and speculating about the nature of the categories needed until we became familiar enough with the material to match content with the relevant categories. The main drawback of this method is that it is very time-consuming; the main advantage is that no prior assumptions are made about the data; *the categories are derived inductively from the data rather than externally imposed.*

The unit identified for analysis was a *statement* — that is, a verbal response whose content (or a major portion of it) could be attributed to a particular topic. Two comments made on a topic at different points in the interview were defined as two separate statements, as were consecutive comments on different topics. Thus if a woman talked about family planning, then moved on to describe her relationship with her husband, and then went back to discussing family planning, three statements were identified for that woman — two on "family planning" and one on "family relations." Once statements were identified, subject categories and subcategories were defined and the verbatim quotes classified. After this was done once, the statements were reread, and the categories and the subcategories were reassessed and in some cases redefined; some statements were reclassified in light of these changes in categories. Only at this point were the statements analyzed in an attempt to quantify women's comments about various subjects. This type of analysis also provides an opportunity to explore some *qualitative* aspects of the responses. For instance, from the number of women responding and the content of their responses, we were able to discern not only which parent — the father or the mother — was most influential in women's pursuit of an education, but also the nature (active or passive) and the success of these parental attempts to influence.

The reader is likely to—and for a number of reasons *should*—find seeming discrepancies between this analysis and Huston's narrative account of her interviews. First, not all of the women who were interviewed are part of this analysis; those women occupying highly visible policymaking positions were *not* included.

---

[1]*For this analysis, women with three or more years of formal schooling were considered "literate"; women with less than three years of formal schooling were considered "illiterate." The judgment of whether a woman was from an "urban" or a "rural" area was made by Perdita Huston.*

[2]*However, the conditions portrayed by the women may be assumed to be accurate if they are substantiated by the findings of further research.*

*Table 1*

**Women in the Sample, by Country, Sector, and Literacy**
**(numbers and percentages)**

| | Rural | | Urban | | Total | | | |
|---|---|---|---|---|---|---|---|---|
| | | | | | | | All Sectors | |
| | Lit. | Illit. | Lit. | Illit. | Rural | Urban | | |
| | (numbers) | | (numbers) | | (numbers) | | (nos.) | (%) |
| Egypt | 2 | 5 | 11 | 3 | 7 | 14 | 21 | 17 |
| Kenya | 5 | 12 | 16 | 5 | 17 | 21 | 38 | 31 |
| Sudan | 4 | 1 | 7 | 1 | 5 | 8 | 13 | 11 |
| Tunisia | 5 | 11 | 2 | 0 | 16 | 2 | 18 | 15 |
| Sri Lanka | 9 | 6 | 4 | 0 | 15 | 4 | 19 | 15 |
| Mexico | 3 | 4 | 6 | 1 | 7 | 7 | 14 | 11 |
| Total | 28 | 39 | 46 | 10 | 67 | 56 | 123 | 100 |
| | | | *(percentages)* | | | | | |
| | *23* | *32* | *37* | *8* | *55* | *45* | *100* | |

NOTES: *Based on information for 118 women, the mean age of women interviewed was 33.5 years; the standard deviation is 12.07. Based on 68 cases, the mean number of children the women had borne was 5.22; the standard deviation is 3.33. Based on information for 101 women, 72 of the women interviewed were married, 24 were single, 2 were widowed, and 3 were divorced.*

Second, the women interviewed usually continued talking after the tape recorder was turned off. During the unrecorded (and therefore not analyzed) portions of conversations, women often communicated more personal thoughts and feelings than they did when they were being taped. (An example of this is provided by Huston's striking finding of the frequency with which women stated that their husbands beat them—even though few statements about wife beating were actually recorded.) Third and most important, this content analysis of the interview material does not pick up—as Huston's own account does—the *intensity* of women's statements; nor does it take account of nonverbal (facial and body) expressions.

## THE THEME OF "CHANGE"

One of the major subjects of discussion—often prompted by the question, "How do you feel your life differed from that of your mother or your grandmother?" —was the ways in which the interviewees' lives differed from those of the women of previous generations. Of the 123 women, 89 made statements about change between past generations and the present. A total of 226 statements about change were identified and coded independently by two female judges who assigned scores of +1 to statements about positive changes, scores of −1 to statements about negative changes, and scores of zero to statements from which it could not be determined whether the change was perceived by the woman making the statement to be beneficial or detrimental. Zero was also used for those statements that attributed *both* positive and negative aspects to the same change. The independent ratings from the two judges were then averaged to obtain a score for each statement. (In many cases, coding was straightforward because words such as "luckily" or "unfortunately" appeared in the statement. In other cases, clue words or phrases were missing, but the nature of the change suggested the appropriate code, e.g., improved hygiene.) Overall, there was a very high degree of agreement between the two judges, indicating that this method of measuring the meaning of change for the population analyzed is highly reliable.[3]

The women perceived change in their lives to have been both beneficial and detrimental. As one rural Mexican woman noted, "Despite advances, women are still poor." Another remark by a rural woman in Sri Lanka captures the dual nature of change very vividly:

"Our land got distributed. Now our portion is very small. This is not sufficient for us to exist. Our mother's generation did not have all the opportunities that we have at the moment—mainly for education, health, transport, and so on. But economically, they were better off because the earlier generation got income that was sufficient to meet all their requirements. Economically, of course, we get much more than what our parents earned. Because of the high cost of living since then, we are not living a happy life. We find life hard."

Of the 226 statements, 136 were positive statements about change, 46 were negative, and 44 were "valueless" in this sense or contained both positive and negative assessments of the same change. The women clearly found some areas of their lives to have been more positively affected by change than others. They found that changes in the areas of education, health, social participation, and political and legal rights have been beneficial. Nearly one third of the women who identified a positive change phrased it in terms of freedom, independence, or gains in political rights and in health and public services. Women's perceptions of change in the area of family relations were mixed. Choice of (or at least prior acquaintance with) prospective spouses and later age at the time of marriage were both identified as positive changes. Husband-wife relations were more often perceived to be deteriorating than to be improving. Less attention to and respect for the elderly and less communication within the extended family also were perceived as negative changes. Some women said they were glad to see children having more freedom in the family while others were concerned about declining parental authority. On the subject of economic change, more than any other type of change, the number of negative statements exceeded the number of positive ones. Women spoke favorably of easier access to out-of-home, remunerated work and of improved standards of living, but the cash economy, higher prices, food shortages, and loss of property ownership were perceived to be inflicting severe hardship.[4]

What do we know about the women who talked about these changes? The percentage of rural (45 per cent) and urban (55 per cent) women who spoke out about change was proportionate to the rural-urban breakdown among the 123 women. The percentage of women who spoke of change who were literate (55 per cent) was slightly smaller than the percentage of literate women in the sample. (See Tables 1 and 2.) Both literate and illiterate and both urban and rural women commented about changes in education and in the economy. Of the 89

---

[3]The Pearson Product Moment Correlation Coefficient between the ratings of the two independent judges was .93.

[4]Not all the categories resulting from the initial classification have yet been analyzed; categories that remain to be analyzed are "religion," "mass media," "politics," "women's organizations," and "International Women's Year." For those who wish to conduct further analyses, the data for these and all other categories are available through the International Center for Research on Women (2000 P Street, N.W., Suite 403, Washington, D.C. 20036). They can only be used at the ICRW offices. The ICRW will not be able to fulfill any mail requests for copies of the data.

*Table 2*
## Women Making Statements About Change
### (numbers and percentages)

| | Rural | | Urban | | Total | | | |
|---|---|---|---|---|---|---|---|---|
| | Lit. | Illit. | Lit. | Illit. | Rural | Urban | All Sectors | |
| | *(numbers)* | | *(numbers)* | | *(numbers)* | | *(nos.)* | *(%)* |
| Egypt | 2 | 4 | 7 | 1 | 6 | 8 | 14 | 16 |
| Kenya | 3 | 10 | 9 | 7 | 13 | 16 | 29 | 33 |
| Sudan | 2 | 1 | 3 | 1 | 3 | 4 | 7 | 8 |
| Tunisia | 3 | 9 | 0 | 0 | 12 | 0 | 12 | 13 |
| Sri Lanka | 9 | 3 | 4 | 0 | 12 | 4 | 16 | 18 |
| Mexico | 0 | 3 | 7 | 1 | 3 | 8 | 11 | 12 |
| Total | 19 | 30 | 30 | 10 | 49 | 40 | 89 | 100 |
| | | | | *(percentages)* | | | | |
| | *21* | *34* | *34* | *11* | *55* | *45* | *100* | |

women who commented on change, 37 found education to have improved. Most of the women who spoke of positive health changes were from rural areas—22 of the 27.

Although many of the same themes emerged over and over again in the statements about change, there were some notable country differences. The comments referring to change made by Tunisian women were overwhelmingly positive—particularly on the subjects of independence, freedom, and political rights. Education was the major positive change cited by Mexican women; Egyptian women referred to social and economic independence. Some of the same themes—educational opportunity, independence, and mobility—were echoed by the Sri Lankan women. Thirty-three (33) per cent of the women who commented on change were Kenyan women (who comprise 31 per cent of the total number interviewed). It is noteworthy that a highly disproportionate number of the total number of negative comments made (33 of 46) were made by these East African women, who were grateful that their children were healthy and better educated, but found changes in family relations, high prices, and the cash economy oppressive. Are these Kenyan women in fact worse off than their counterparts in other countries?

A majority of women's statements, while not specifically related to change, shed light on why the women perceive their situations to have improved or deteriorated. Figure 1 shows that women made statements that can be grouped into six major categories or themes. They made statements about economic conditions; family relations; education; health, nutrition, and family planning; their perceptions of themselves, of men, and of other women; and their aspirations. Within these major themes, women's statements were grouped further into subcategories or subthemes. More women talked about economic conditions than about any other topics—suggesting the importance of economic variables in their lives. Next, they talked about their perceptions of themselves and others, health and family planning, and their relationships with their families. The

*Figure 1*

## Rank Ordering of Themes and Subthemes Expressed by 123 Women

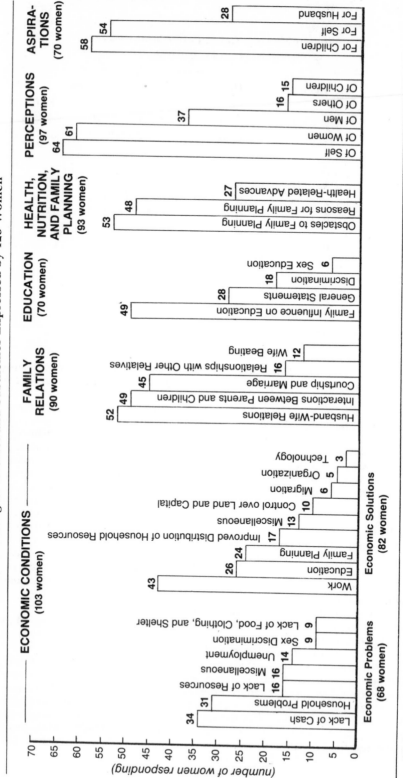

NOTE: Within any subtheme (e.g., lack of cash), a woman was counted only once, even if she made several statements about that subtheme. Theme totals (e.g., economic conditions) include each woman only once, even if she made comments in all subthemes. Therefore theme totals do not correspond to the sum of their subtheme totals.

following sections discuss the women's statements, identifying the women expressing particular sentiments as urban or rural, literate or illiterate. The sections below summarize the analysis of the major subject categories; each section includes those statements specifically on change as well as all other statements related to the subject.

## ECONOMIC CONDITIONS

Statements related to the economy and to women's perceptions about the economy were analyzed to determine both what the women considered to be their major problems and their proposed solutions to these problems. Sixty-eight women made 172 statements related to economic problems, and 82 women made 200 statements suggesting needed solutions to economic problems. It is interesting to observe that *solutions* to economic problems — rather than economic *problems* per se — were mentioned more often and by more women. Thirty-seven urban and 31 rural, 46 literate and 22 illiterate women talked about economic problems. Forty urban and 42 rural, 49 literate and 33 illiterate women mentioned solutions to economic problems. (See Table 3.)

### *Statements Describing Economic Problems*

The economic problems category contains those statements in which women indicate some difficulty in meeting their own, their families', their communities', or women's (in general) economic needs. These problem statements are divided into several subcategories.

*Lack of Cash.* More statements about economic problems focused on the lack of cash than on any other issue. Compared with their proportions in the population interviewed, slightly higher percentages of urban (48 per cent) and literate (64 per cent) women mentioned economic problems related to the absence of available cash. Women from Kenya made these statements most often; 17 of the 34 women who spoke about lack of cash were Kenyan women. This problem of lack of money frequently was linked explicitly to the inability to satisfy such essential needs as food, health care, and education. Women discussing the high cost of living and inflation were primarily from rural areas; these women often associated the high cost of living with a difficult, complicated, unhappy life. The change from a subsistence to a cash economy has not always been advantageous to women. Women often stated that, in contrast to today, money previously was not needed to purchase food or to satisfy other basic needs and that women's work — in farming, in handicrafts, or within the household — does not bring enough money or any money at all.

*Household Problems.* Of the women who commented about the relationship between economic problems and the household situation, more were urban (55 per cent) and literate (71 per cent) than rural and illiterate. (Of the total numbers of women interviewed, 45 per cent were urban and 60 per cent were literate.) In a third of the statements about this relationship, women complained that men spend their earned income on themselves and do not share it with the family. Of the 11 statements made about this problem, 9 were made by rural and 2 by urban women. Most of these women were illiterate.

Women also mentioned the strains associated with the double roles of working both within and outside the household. One woman stated: "I work in the field, opposite the men, seven hours of hard work, and then I go home, and I am required to play the role of a housewife 100 per cent—cooking, cleaning, and washing for the children." Another woman stated: "I am working outside and inside. I am doing a dual job. Some people think that work is liberation of women. It is not liberation. Sometimes it is just that women are more exploited."

135

*Table 3*

**Women Making Statements About Economic Problems
and Proposed Solutions
(numbers and percentages)**

| | Rural | | Urban | | Total | | | |
|---|---|---|---|---|---|---|---|---|
| | Lit. | Illit. | Lit. | Illit. | Rural | Urban | All Sectors | |
| | *(numbers)* | | *(numbers)* | | *(numbers)* | | *(nos.)* | *(%)* |
| | | | | ECONOMIC PROBLEMS | | | | |
| Egypt | 1 | 0 | 8 | 0 | 1 | 8 | 9 | 13 |
| Kenya | 5 | 9 | 12 | 5 | 14 | 17 | 31 | 46 |
| Sudan | 3 | 0 | 1 | 0 | 3 | 1 | 4 | 6 |
| Tunisia | 1 | 1 | 1 | 0 | 2 | 1 | 3 | 4 |
| Sri Lanka | 3 | 2 | 4 | 0 | 5 | 4 | 9 | 13 |
| Mexico | 2 | 4 | 5 | 1 | 6 | 6 | 12 | 18 |
| Total | 15 | 16 | 31 | 6 | 31 | 37 | 68 | 100 |
| | | | | *(percentages)* | | | | |
| | *22* | *24* | *45* | *9* | *46* | *54* | *100* | |
| | | | | ECONOMIC SOLUTIONS | | | | |
| Egypt | 1 | 4 | 10 | 0 | 5 | 10 | 15 | 18 |
| Kenya | 3 | 9 | 14 | 5 | 12 | 19 | 31 | 38 |
| Sudan | 3 | 1 | 3 | 1 | 4 | 4 | 8 | 10 |
| Tunisia | 2 | 4 | 0 | 0 | 6 | 0 | 6 | 7 |
| Sri Lanka | 5 | 5 | 4 | 0 | 10 | 4 | 14 | 17 |
| Mexico | 2 | 3 | 2 | 1 | 5 | 3 | 8 | 10 |
| Total | 16 | 26 | 33 | 7 | 42 | 40 | 82 | 100 |
| | | | | *(percentages)* | | | | |
| | *19* | *32* | *40* | *9* | *51* | *49* | *100* | |

*Lack of Resources.* The phrase "lack of resources" refers to those statements describing the absence of such resources as land, capital, and the machines necessary for production, and the lack of markets for the exchange of goods and services produced. Land is the resource most frequently mentioned as lacking, especially by women in Kenya; 10 of the 16 women who mentioned lack of resources were Kenyan.

*Unemployment.* The women perceive unemployment to be a general economic problem, not one specific to women. Unemployment was mentioned as a problem by more literate than illiterate (11 versus 3) women and more urban than rural (9 versus 5) women. It is quite probable that because literate and urban women have more wage-employment options than illiterate and/or rural women, they are more aware of the lack of jobs. A repeated complaint was that, even with an education, women cannot find jobs. This seems to suggest that education in its present form is not appropriate for the demands of the job market in the city, and that widespread education alone may not be the answer to massive economic problems.

*Sex Discrimination.* Sex discrimination — including general job discrimination, lower salaries for women, exploitation of female workers by men, and lack of promotions for women — were perceived to be a problem primarily by educated urban women. Statements of 9 educated women indict men as exploiters: "Women are bullied by their [male] bosses," and "He put her at home and began feeding her and deprived her of paid work."

*Lack of Food, Clothing, and Shelter.* Nine women — eight of them Kenyan women — explicitly commented about the lack of satisfaction of food, clothing, and shelter needs. Seven of the Kenyan women live in rural areas; their comments primarily were about the lack of sufficient food to feed themselves and/or their families: "I don't have anything to eat like it was before," and "Nowadays we don't have enough grain, so you can see our things are not doing well."

### Statements Proposing Solutions to Economic Problems

More women mentioned potential *solutions* to stated or implied economic problems than mentioned economic *problems.* Rural and urban, literate and illiterate women were represented in this category in the proportions they comprised among the 123 women. As in the economic problems category, Kenyan women responded in greatest numbers; 31 of the 38 Kenyan women interviewed suggested one or more solutions to economic problems.

*Work.* Women want work that will bring in cash. In 50 of the 75 statements in this subcategory, women made reference to the wage sector of the economy, indicating that they see employment as a major vehicle for resolving their economic problems. The desire or need for a profession was the second largest work subcategory, with 23 statements; teaching, nursing, office work, and midwifery were the most frequently mentioned professions. Eleven statements were made (mostly by rural women) expressing a desire to participate in setting up business enterprises, in trade, and in marketing activities. Rural women also mentioned handicrafts and agricultural production as means of bettering their lives.

*Education.* The 26 women who suggested education as one way of dealing with economic problems proportionately represented urban (46 per cent) and rural (54 per cent), literate (61 per cent) and illiterate (39 per cent) women interviewed. Literacy was not seen by these women as a direct means of increasing their economic productivity. Instead, the women said they wanted educational opportunities that would lead directly to income generation; they see a need for training in agricultural techniques, handicrafts, technical skills, marketing, and business. Only 5 of the women who spoke about education as a potential solution to economic problems considered it the sole answer to economic problems; all others cited education as only one of several needed solutions.

*Family Planning.* Urban and rural women were represented in this subcategory (11 and 13 women, respectively) in proportion to their representation among the 123 women. Although more literate than illiterate women were interviewed, more illiterate (14) than literate (10) women commented on family planning as a potential solution to economic problems. Women in Kenya and Egypt most often cited family planning as an answer to economic difficulties — especially as a way to lessen the problem of lack of food. They also perceived family planning as an aid to providing their children with a better education and to improving both immediate and future family and personal well-being.

*Distribution of Household Resources.* Relative to their proportion in the population interviewed, slightly more urban than rural women suggested that better distribution of the household's resources would be one way to address economic problems (10 of the 17 women commenting in this subcategory were from urban areas). It may be that city life produces more family strains or increases these women's expectations of the family's economic responsibilities. Ten women wished for their husbands to provide more resources, to contribute to the family income, to permit their wives to work, and to allow their wives economic independence. The women also expressed a need for child-care centers to ease the burdens on women playing the double role of mother and worker.

*Control over Land and Capital.* Of the 10 women who spoke of their need to gain control over resources, 7 were from rural areas and 6 were illiterate. Eight of the 10 women referred to resources related to agriculture (land, seeds, and grinding mills). Two women expressed the need for capital. These rural women apparently perceived the control of resources and the means of production as a more viable alternative for improving their economic situation than working for wages.

*Migration.* Migration was suggested as a solution to economic problems by 6 women. Still fewer women (3) mentioned *technology* as a response to economic problems. All these women were urban and saw technology primarily as a tool for increasing household production.

## FAMILY RELATIONS

The other major area of change about which women spoke mainly in negative terms was "family relations." In making statements describing changes in interactions among family members over the past generation, the women expressed positive feelings about changes in several areas — e.g., the process of courtship and marriage, including the opportunity of choosing, or at least of getting to know prior to marriage, one's marital partner, and the tendency to marry at a somewhat later age — but they expressed negative feelings about changes in other areas — e.g., deteriorating relationships with their husbands.

In this category, 254 statements were made by 90 women. Compared to their proportions in the population interviewed, slightly more urban and literate women made statements describing relations among members of the family. (See Tables 1 and 4.)

*Husband-Wife Relations.* Of the 39 women who described husband-wife interactions in either positive or negative (rather than neutral) terms, 24 described them negatively. There appeared to be no differences in the frequency with which rural and urban, or literate and illiterate women described such negative interactions. There were, however, country differences. In Kenya, 11 of the 12 women who spoke about husband-wife relations did so in negative terms. Such country-differentiated findings can at most be used to raise an additional set of questions. In this case, for example, can it be inferred that husband-wife interactions in Kenya really are more negative than in other countries? Or do Kenyan women simply feel more free to talk about this topic? Or do they perhaps have higher expectations of what husband-wife relationships should be and therefore feel more disappointed by a less-than-ideal situation?

About what aspects of their relationships with their husbands did the women interviewed have negative feelings? The statements indicate that conflicts between men and women had arisen over women's nontraditional work, educational, and social roles (7 women), as well as over child-care and household tasks (6 women). Also mentioned were conflicts over the sexual aspects of marriage, disputes about the household budget, and women's lack of domestic authority and power. Twenty-two women expressed views about who has

138

*Table 4*
## Women Making Statements About Family Relations
### (numbers and percentages)

| | Rural | | Urban | | Total | | | |
|---|---|---|---|---|---|---|---|---|
| | Lit. | Illit. | Lit. | Illit. | Rural | Urban | All Sectors | |
| | (numbers) | | (numbers) | | (numbers) | | (nos.) | (%) |
| Egypt | 2 | 2 | 9 | 3 | 4 | 12 | 16 | 18 |
| Kenya | 3 | 8 | 11 | 5 | 11 | 16 | 27 | 30 |
| Sudan | 4 | 0 | 6 | 0 | 4 | 6 | 10 | 11 |
| Tunisia | 5 | 7 | 1 | 0 | 12 | 1 | 13 | 15 |
| Sri Lanka | 5 | 3 | 4 | 0 | 8 | 4 | 12 | 13 |
| Mexico | 3 | 2 | 6 | 1 | 5 | 7 | 12 | 13 |
| | 22 | 22 | 37 | 9 | 44 | 46 | 90 | 100 |
| | | | (percentages) | | | | | |
| | 24 | 25 | 41 | 10 | 49 | 51 | 100 | |

decision-making prerogatives in husband-wife interactions; 16 of them perceived the *husband* to have control and authority in the husband-wife relationship, 4 women mentioned that both partners share in the authority, and only 2 mentioned that the woman has control in the relationship.

More than half of the 15 women who viewed husband-wife interactions positively expressed these interactions in terms of the sharing of tasks by husband and wife and in terms of respect and understanding between husband and wife. Married women's expressions of what they would like from their husbands also were phrased most often in terms of the sharing of household decisions and responsibilities. It seems that women wanted more equal husband-wife roles but perceived the men to have the upper hand in marital relationships. Twenty-eight women described what an ideal husband would be like. Urban women most frequently identified "good character" (i.e., a husband who is honest and has high moral principles) as a desirable trait, while rural women emphasized education, hard work, and sobriety.

*Interactions Between Parents and Children.* The specific point most frequently made by the 49 women in this category related to how their parents had been influential in shaping their personality and social development. Of the 31 women who described such parental influence, 17 saw their fathers as having had a positive influence in their personality and social development, and 11 thought of their mothers as having played the same role. Five women mentioned their fathers and 9 women mentioned their mothers as having had a negative influence on them. There was no urban/rural difference in the distribution of these comments.

What kinds of supportive influence did fathers and mothers have on their daughters? The women's statements about parental influence were classified into those showing passive or active influence. Positive statements about parental influence — phrased in terms of emotional support or affection — were said to

represent *passive* parental influence; statements revealing that parents motivated the woman to do something specific were called *active* parental influence
statements. Ten women referred to their fathers' positive influence in *active*
terms; in contrast, 8 women referred to their mothers' positive influence as
*passive*. Thus mothers were perceived to have given love and affection, while
fathers were considered to have taught and motivated their daughters. Of the 9
women who mentioned their mothers' negative influence, 6 mentioned mothers
having used passive love withdrawal to exercise influence. In contrast, 4 of the 5
women mentioned their fathers as having actively opposed something they
wanted to do.

*Courtship and Marriage.* Of the 45 women who made statements related to
this category, 20 mentioned how their marital partners had been chosen; 13 of
them stated that they themselves had chosen their husbands. A Sri Lankan
woman who had done a survey of urban working-class women stated that she
had found that roughly 50 per cent of the women surveyed had chosen their own
spouses. She further stated: "I wouldn't say it's the traditional arranged marriages completely breaking down, but the two systems seem to be surviving
independently and not coming into conflict."

The women gave no single prevalent reason for deciding to marry. They
mentioned love, fulfillment, and respect, among other reasons, suggesting that
they perhaps have more choice about *who* they marry than about *whether* they
marry. Nor was there a common perception of what it takes to make an ideal
marriage.

*Wife Beating.* Eleven women made *recorded* comments about wife beating.
(Huston indicates elsewhere in this volume that many women made such comments at points when she was not taping.) In speaking about why husbands beat
their wives, 2 women cited differences over money, 3 mentioned drunkenness,
and 6 cited the wives' "misbehavior." Referring to society's sanction of wife
beating, one woman said, "Nothing happens—because it is between you, your
husband, and your family."

## EDUCATION

Although the women perceived changes in the areas of economics and family
relations to have been primarily negative, they considered the changes that had
taken place in the areas of education, health, and social relations to be positive.
All but 3 out of 40 statements about change in the area of education were positive
statements. Seventy women made statements about education. Higher percentages of these were urban and literate (56 and 64 per cent, respectively) than was
true of the entire population interviewed. (See Table 5.) Women said their lives
were better because they were better educated than their mothers and grand-
mothers and because their children and people in general have increased access
to more education. Development's contribution to this change is obvious: it has
provided the infrastructure for education (i.e., more schools, roads, etc.). But in
developing countries, boys still tend to go to (and stay in) school more often than
girls. One of the many variables that may explain this difference is who motivates
the child to receive an education.

*Family Influence on Education.* The topic most frequently mentioned in the
education category was who had the most influence in motivating women to
pursue an education. Forty-nine women talked about who had influenced their
pursuit of an education — often in response to the question, "What was your
family's influence on your education?" Thirty-four women mentioned one or
both parents as having influenced them. Only 4 of the 34 women were illiterate;
16 lived in rural areas and 18 in urban areas. Twenty-four of these women
mentioned their fathers as having had an influence—either positive or negative
—on their education; this influence was described as positive by 14 women and as

140

*Table 5*
## Women Making Statements About Education
### (numbers and percentages)

| | Rural Lit. (numbers) | Rural Illit. (numbers) | Urban Lit. (numbers) | Urban Illit. (numbers) | Total Rural (numbers) | Total Urban (numbers) | Total All Sectors (nos.) | Total All Sectors (%) |
|---|---|---|---|---|---|---|---|---|
| Egypt | 1 | 3 | 10 | 2 | 4 | 12 | 16 | 23 |
| Kenya | 2 | 6 | 13 | 2 | 8 | 15 | 23 | 33 |
| Sudan | 3 | 1 | 3 | 0 | 4 | 3 | 7 | 10 |
| Tunisia | 4 | 8 | 1 | 0 | 12 | 1 | 13 | 19 |
| Sri Lanka | 1 | 1 | 3 | 1 | 2 | 4 | 6 | 8 |
| Mexico | 1 | 0 | 3 | 1 | 1 | 4 | 5 | 7 |
| Total | 12 | 19 | 33 | 6 | 31 | 39 | 70 | 100 |
| *(percentages)* | 17 | 27 | 47 | 9 | 44 | 56 | | 100 |

negative by 10. Seven women spoke of their mothers' influence on their education in negative terms, and 6 women did so in positive terms.

In each of the countries and in both rural and urban situations, women perceived that their fathers exerted a predominant influence — whether supportive or not — on their education. Regardless of the accuracy of the women's perceptions of their parents' influence, the hypothesis that fathers played a central role in the women's education is supported by the fact that 3 of the 4 illiterate women mentioned their fathers as having prevented them from going to school, while all of the women who described their mothers as having had a negative influence on their education were in fact *literate* women. Women most often spoke of their fathers' *positive* influence as having actively encouraged them to break with tradition and pursue an education. In many cases, the fathers themselves had received an education. The fathers' influence thus seems to have been transmitted to the daughters directly, through teaching and encouragement, as well as indirectly, by providing a role model to be imitated. Women most often spoke of their fathers' *negative* influence as having been conveyed by insistence that education is not necessary for—and perhaps is even antithetical to —a daughter's future role as homemaker and childbearer. One woman said that her father thought education encouraged permissiveness in women: "Girls who go to school get pregnant." The positive influence of mothers generally was described in terms of having taught their daughters appropriate sex-role norms and behaviors, both in personal matters (i.e., how to be a "good girl") and in the work sphere (i.e., housework and child-care skills).

*Educational Aspirations.*[5] Whether or not they themselves were literate, all the women who commented on education expressed the belief that education of-

---

[5]*Table 6 provides a breakdown of the women making statements about their aspirations in general (i.e., not just about education). The women's aspirations are defined as their expressions of future goals for themselves or for others.*

*Table 6*

**Women Making Statements About Their Aspirations**
**(numbers and percentages)**

| | Rural | | Urban | | Total | | | |
|---|---|---|---|---|---|---|---|---|
| | Lit. | Illit. | Lit. | Illit. | Rural | Urban | All Sectors | |
| | *(numbers)* | | *(numbers)* | | *(numbers)* | | *(nos.)* | *(%)* |
| Egypt | 2 | 1 | 2 | 3 | 3 | 5 | 8 | 11 |
| Kenya | 4 | 5 | 9 | 5 | 9 | 14 | 23 | 33 |
| Sudan | 6 | 1 | 3 | 1 | 7 | 4 | 11 | 16 |
| Tunisia | 4 | 9 | 0 | 0 | 13 | 0 | 13 | 19 |
| Sri Lanka | 5 | 3 | 1 | 0 | 8 | 1 | 9 | 13 |
| Mexico | 1 | 1 | 3 | 1 | 2 | 4 | 6 | 8 |
| Total | 22 | 20 | 18 | 10 | 42 | 28 | 70 | 100 |
| | | | *(percentages)* | | | | | |
| | *31* | *29* | *26* | *14* | *60* | *40* | *100* | |

fered advantages. Thirty-nine of the 54 women who spoke of their own aspirations said they wanted to acquire an education. The rest wanted a variation of this — they wanted to acquire skills that would require only minimum training but would enable them to work for pay; a majority of these women were from the rural areas. Among those who wanted formal educational training, the careers identified as desirable varied from teaching to being a prison guard. About half of the women wanted to be teachers; 12 expressed an interest in medical careers — half of them wanting to be doctors, the other half, nurses. The major reason given for pursuing a formal education was the desire to be able to provide useful services to others. Few perceived education as an end in itself.

The women identified education as an aspiration they held for their children as well as for themselves. Forty-one of the 58 women who talked about their aspirations for their children identified education as a major priority. The women were concerned that children obtain the education, training, or skills that will help them to get good jobs. They most frequently wanted their children to become teachers and doctors. Only one woman mentioned that she wanted her children to be farmers.

## HEALTH, NUTRITION, AND FAMILY PLANNING

Twenty-seven women explicitly mentioned that their lives were better than those of their parents because of the health-related advances that had taken place. Twenty-two of these women were from rural areas and most of them were illiterate. Better availability of health services, along with improved general health, nutrition, and hygiene, were the most frequently mentioned positive health changes. (Additional comments on health and nutrition were so scattered as to make it impossible to further analyze statements in these categories.) The availability of modern contraceptives was the next most frequently mentioned positive change in health. Women had divided opinions about what actually had happened to family size. But whether they perceive family size to have increased or decreased in the last generation, they considered smaller families to be more desirable. Of the women interviewed, 68 gave information on the size of their families; the average number of children these women had borne was 5.2. Seventy-six women commented on obstacles to family planning and/or on reasons for planning their families. (See Table 7).

*Obstacles to Family Planning.* Fifty-three women gave reasons why they or other women in their countries were unwilling to control their fertility. Concern about the side effects of contraceptives was the reason mentioned most often; 21 women talked about negative side effects of contraceptives that they either knew about first-hand or about which they had heard. Other reasons, in order of importance, were the opposition of their husbands (13 women), religious or superstitious beliefs (12 women), problems with the health delivery system (10 women), and societal disapproval (10 women). Two women mentioned that children provide future economic security to the parents.

The women citing obstacles to family planning reflected the distribution of rural and urban, literate and illiterate women among the 123 women interviewed. Concern about the physical side effects of contraceptives was shared by women in all six countries. The birth control pill was associated with headaches and fainting, the intrauterine device with bleeding and loss of weight. The IUD appeared to be the most feared device for controlling fertility. Some women were afraid that the inserted IUD would move within the body and get lost. One woman said, for instance, "I am afraid that the coil would get lost and come through on the other side of my head."

Mexican women identified opposition by local priests as the main obstacle to family planning. In addition, Mexican women said they had to deal with their husbands' opposition. The women said they believed that the men object to

*Table 7*
### Women Making Statements About Family Planning
### (numbers and percentages)

| | Rural | | Urban | | Total | | | |
|---|---|---|---|---|---|---|---|---|
| | Lit. | Illit. | Lit. | Illit. | Rural | Urban | All Sectors | |
| | *(numbers)* | | *(numbers)* | | *(numbers)* | | *(nos.)* | *(%)* |
| Egypt | 0 | 1 | 8 | 1 | 1 | 9 | 10 | 13 |
| Kenya | 4 | 7 | 8 | 6 | 11 | 14 | 25 | 33 |
| Sudan | 3 | 0 | 3 | 1 | 3 | 4 | 7 | 9 |
| Tunisia | 1 | 8 | 1 | 0 | 9 | 1 | 10 | 13 |
| Sri Lanka | 7 | 3 | 3 | 0 | 10 | 3 | 13 | 17 |
| Mexico | 2 | 3 | 6 | 0 | 5 | 6 | 11 | 15 |
| Total | 17 | 22 | 29 | 8 | 39 | 37 | 76 | 100 |
| | | | | *(percentages)* | | | | |
| | 22 | 29 | 38 | 11 | 51 | 49 | 100 | |

family planning for two major reasons: fear of the physical side effects of the birth control devices, particularly that the devices will sterilize their wives; and fear that their wives will become sexually permissive. A Tunisian woman said that her husband objects to her use of contraceptives because, he says, "It isn't normal to avoid the life that you are destined to live." She said he told her that woman is "like the chicken, with a certain number of eggs to lay—it would be a sin not to lay them." Despite her husband's objections, this forty-year-old woman, who had already given birth to ten children, had obtained an IUD.

Some women said that their husbands did not permit them to get IUDs because they did not want them to be examined by a male doctor. In the words of one Egyptian woman, "In the rural sector, there was no question of a man examining a woman. She would not go, the husband would not allow it." A Kenyan woman said she believed that men wanted their wives to bear children so that they would stay at home. She said, "The men could not care less about family planning—you never see a man going to a family planning clinic. Some, I think, would like to have more children to keep the women at home." A social worker in Sri Lanka, on the other hand, described the other side of the picture, observing that some women refuse contraceptives because they think that children will keep the men at home.

Some women said that those who want to plan the spacing of their children often face societal and family pressures to bear children. A rural Tunisian woman who had given birth to eight children told of her own experience of such pressure: "All the women made fun of me. They reproached me for getting an IUD, but I decided to get one, and I did." Another Tunisian woman, a mother of four, said that when she got an IUD, her mother-in-law said, "We have only one son. Why do you want to stop your pregnancies?" Women in Sri Lanka mentioned cultural pressures to bear sons and the inferior status of childless couples. Sudanese women also indicated that they are subjected to cultural pressures to have large families. In fact, according to one woman, "the women who have had more children will get a medal."

*Reasons for Family Planning.* Despite the obstacles cited, 48 women gave reasons for planning one's family. Thirty-nine of these women gave economic considerations as a primary reason for limiting family size. These women said that it is better to have fewer children so that they can be better clothed, better fed, and better educated. In expressing their views about planning their families, the women seemed to be less concerned about themselves than about their ability to provide for their children. When they did speak about themselves, it was in terms of their health and the fact that child spacing would give them strength. Unfortunately, no data are available on how many of the women interviewed actually practice family planning.

## PERCEPTIONS[6]

The women interviewed not only shared their feelings about the changes in their lives and their hopes for their families, but also provided glimpses of how they feel about themselves, about other women, and about men. The women's "perceptions" are defined as their views, images, or opinions of themselves or others.

*Self-Perceptions.* Images people have of themselves in different situations and in performing different roles all contribute to their self-identity. Two important, related images or components of the self are how people see themselves as individuals (self-image) and as females or males (sex-role image). The women interviewed discussed both their own personality features and behavioral traits (i.e., "I am a brave woman," "My life is fruitful," "I am unhappy")

---

[6]*Table 8 provides a breakdown of the number of women in this category.*

144

*Table 8*
### Women Making Statements About Perceptions
### (numbers and percentages)

| | Rural | | Urban | | Total | | | |
|---|---|---|---|---|---|---|---|---|
| | | | | | | | All Sectors | |
| | Lit. | Illit. | Lit. | Illit. | Rural | Urban | | |
| | *(numbers)* | | *(numbers)* | | *(numbers)* | | *(nos.)* | *(%)* |
| Egypt | 2 | 4 | 9 | 3 | 6 | 12 | 18 | 19 |
| Kenya | 3 | 9 | 11 | 5 | 12 | 16 | 28 | 29 |
| Sudan | 4 | 1 | 4 | 1 | 5 | 5 | 10 | 10 |
| Tunisia | 5 | ·9 | 1 | 0 | 14 | 1 | 15 | 15 |
| Sri Lanka | 8 | 4 | 4 | 0 | 12 | 4 | 16 | 17 |
| Mexico | 3 | 2 | 4 | 1 | 5 | 5 | 10 | 10 |
| Total | 25 | 29 | 33 | 10 | 54 | 43 | 97 | 100 |
| | | | | *(percentages)* | | | | |
| | *26* | *30* | *34* | *10* | *56* | *44* | *100* | |

and whether or not they would rather have been born male. The former statements were identified as contributing to these women's self-image, the latter as contributing to their sex-role image. A total of 64 women talked about their perceptions of themselves.

Of the 17 women who described characteristics having to do with their self-image, 12 perceived themselves positively. There were no apparent rural-urban differences in the responses falling into this category. Most of the 12 women were literate. Moreover, the 5 women who expressed negative images of themselves were illiterate. These results are probably the effect of self-selection and of the desire to impress an interviewer perceived to be of high status. Despite these biases, it is quite conceivable that education contributes to people's (and perhaps specifically to women's) positive views of themselves.

Of the 49 women who made statements about their sex-role image, half revealed positive feelings and half expressed negative ones. In this case, rural-urban distinctions rather than education seemed to be related to women's responses. Similar numbers of rural and urban women expressed positive views of their sex roles; however, of those women indicating a negative perception of their sex-role identity, 20 live in rural areas. These women wished they had been born male instead of female for two major reasons. First, they would have had less work, fewer responsibilities, and greater mobility and freedom (2 women said that they would have preferred to be male because they would have had the freedom to stay in their place of birth rather than moving to their husband's home). Second, they would have had the education and the privileges, power, and authority that men have. These results suggest that sex roles may be more clearly defined and separated in rural than in urban areas and that this definition of roles works against women. Women perceive that they bear all the burdens and responsibilities of family and work and have none of the benefits that men have. It seems that women are cognizant of and wish for those things in life that society reserves for men only. (It is interesting that rural women complained about their condition only indirectly, in terms of a wish.)

*Perceptions of Women.* Sixty-one women expressed their opinions of other women. Twenty-three commented on women's social character and 30 on their sex-role image. The views expressed were strikingly positive. Sixteen of the women described other women as having attributes that contribute to a positive social character, e.g., women are sincere, honest, patient, persistent. Seven women expressed negative views of other women, saying that women are immoral, gossipy, and quarrelsome. A majority viewed women as being either equal to or better than men, saying, for example, "Woman is as capable as man," or "She is more psychologically mature, clever, and broad-minded."

*Perceptions of Men.* While the women's perception of other women were generally positive, their perceptions of men were not. Of the 37 women who discussed their perceptions of men, 34 described men's social character; of those, 23 did so in negative terms. By far the most common complaint was that men are women's oppressors: they do not regard women as people, they are jealous and selfish, they regard women as servants and as children to be beaten. The women also stated that men are lazy and do not help with housework and child care, and that they are not responsible to the family. In a majority of the cases, perceptions of men were complaints about men's traditional superior place in society.

## CONCLUSIONS

The 123 women interviewed see modernization, industrialization, and urbanization—that is, fast and profound social and economic changes—as having had both positive and negative effects on their lives.

In recent years, scholars have argued that socio-economic development more often than not has had a negative or adverse impact on the lives of women. The women interviewed, however, generally described the changes they have experienced in quite positive rather than in negative terms. Are these two positions — one generated by studying the effects of changes, the other by experiencing them first hand — contradictory? Are the results obtained by objective assessments of the effects of development on people inconsistent with people's perceptions of how development changes have affected them? It may be that the women interviewed by Huston were exceptional in this sense, and that, if she had interviewed a more representative sample, the results would have been different. Or perhaps the women were not stating their real feelings. However, even if these women's feelings are representative of the majority of developing country women's perceptions of change in their lives, the results still may not be contradictory. The thrust and strength of the "negative impact" thesis is *economic.* Development experts often export, along with aid and technology, their beliefs about women and women's roles in society. They often see women only as homemakers and childbearers and consequently implement programs that give the benefits of technology and aid to the men. Yet in many Third World societies, women have roles that extend far beyond homemaking and childbearing. As a result of such development efforts, economic roles — in subsistence agriculture, in commerce, and in some manufacturing industries — that traditionally have been enacted mainly by women or have been shared by many men and women frequently have been reassigned to men, thereby undermining women's economic power and widening the gap between women's and men's earnings.[7] The economic argument does not imply that *all* changes have been negative. The question that cannot be answered here (since it was not possible to

---

[7]*See, for instance, Ester Boserup,* Women's Role in Economic Development *(New York: St. Martin's Press, 1970), and Irene Tinker and Michèle Bo Bramsen, eds.,* Women and World Development, *Vol. 1 (Washington, D.C.: Overseas Development Council, 1976).*

quantify the intensity of the responses) is how much positive health and social changes outweigh negative economic changes—at least in terms of women's own perceived well-being.

## The Experience of Economic Change

The economic category contained more statements by more women than any other category. It seems quite clear that economic conditions affect these women directly and are salient in their minds. Consistent with the negative impact thesis, the women say that they have not benefited greatly from economic changes. The share of negative statements about change was higher in the economic category than in any other category.

The analysis of the statements about economic problems shows that the women perceived deterioration in the economic environment to be the cause of increased complexity and difficulty in their lives. Both urban and rural women stated that the lack of cash is their main economic problem, followed by problems in the distribution of household resources. Unemployment is a problem for urban women, and lack of such vital resources as land is a problem for rural women. However, urban and rural women proposed similar solutions to economic problems, and in the same order of priority: the opportunity to work for pay, education that would lead to employment, and access to family planning in order to be able to distribute the resources more evenly within the household and to provide better education for the children. The women perceived themselves as having primary responsibility for the economic well-being of their families. They did not question the appropriateness of women working for pay outside the household, nor did they say that they expect men to be the main economic providers. These women saw *themselves* as responsible for solving their economic needs — provided that society gives them the opportunity to participate in income-generating economic activities.

## The Experience of Social Change

Change has not only affected the economic options of the women interviewed; it has also affected their private and social lives — many times positively. It has provided them with more education and better health services. The rural women in particular said they feel the positive effects on their lives of better health services. A world of actual or perceived choices and opportunities are newly open to women, who now have more freedom to choose a husband, a career, a contraceptive.

The analysis of the women's statements about educational levels and educational aspirations reveals not only the emphasis they place on education as the single most important road for advancement, but also the central role fathers play in helping these women to find and follow this road. In fact, fathers were perceived to have a more active and influential role than mothers—both in their daughters' educational pursuits *and* in their social and personality development. Education today, however, is no guarantee of upward mobility and access to income, especially for those women who continue to pursue "traditional" female jobs that are low in demand and high in supply. (The frustration these women— and their children—may suffer if the effort and money spent on education do not pay off may turn out to be a severe setback for the advancement of women.)

## A Hypothesis for a Country Difference

The analysis of the women's statements suggests that the Kenyan women's perceptions were different from those of the other women. Kenyan women, more than the others, felt that the effects of economic change had been negative; they also described husband-wife interactions in negative terms most frequently. Do these findings suggest that the Kenyan women are really worse off than their counterparts in other countries? Women always have played a central role in the economy of Kenya; 80 per cent of subsistence agriculture still is in the hands of women. This traditional central economic role probably had an "equalizing" impact on the interactions between husbands and wives. As modernization and development have strengthened men's role at the expense of women's in the economic sphere, Kenyan women may have lost some of their rights or prerogatives vis-à-vis their husbands. Perhaps their negative perception of the impact of economic change on husband-wife interactions does not reflect that they are in absolute terms worse off than other women, but that they used to be better off.

The women interviewed were willing to express—to a woman interviewer—not only their problems, but also their aspirations for a better life for themselves and their families and their willingness to work toward actualizing these aspirations. Their many and resourceful views on solutions to economic problems show that they feel *responsible* for the economic welfare of the family, know what should be done to improve the family's economic situation, and wish to integrate themselves into the economy of their communities and countries so they can better provide for their families. The women appear to have the *motivation* to better their lives—a key factor for the success of development efforts. The fact that the rural and illiterate are as able as the urban and literate women to articulate and communicate their problems, needs, hopes, and opinions is useful for policymakers to know. The myth that the rural or illiterate woman is not aware of what is happening around her and is not able to articulate her needs remains, at least for these women, simply that: a myth.

ANNEX B

SOCIAL AND ECONOMIC INDICATORS
OF DEVELOPMENT

## Table 1
### Economic and Social Indicators of Development

| | Population[a] (thousands) | Rate of Natural Increase[b] (per cent) | Per Capita GNP, 1976 ($) | Per Capita GNP Growth Rate, 1970-75 (per cent) | Physical Quality of Life Index (PQLI)[c][d] | Life Expectancy[c][e] (years) | Infant Mortality per 1,000 Live Births[c] | Literacy[c] (per cent) |
|---|---|---|---|---|---|---|---|---|
| Egypt | 36,656 | 2.5 | 280 | 1.3 | 44 | 58 | 108 | 26 |
| Female | 17,957 | | | | 39 | 60 | 115 | 9 |
| Male | 18,698 | | | | 45 | 57 | 104 | 32 |
| Kenya | 10,942 | 3.3 | 240 | 2.4 | 39 | 56 | 119 | 20-25 |
| Female | 5,460 | | | | 37 | 57 | 112 | 10 |
| Male | 5,482 | | | | 38 | 53 | 126 | 30 |
| Sudan | 14,171 | 3.1 | 290 | 3.8 | 34 | 56 | 141 | 15 |
| Tunisia | 5,588 | 2.3 | 840 | 6.9 | 46 | 63 | 135 | 32 |
| Female | 2,747 | | | | | | | |
| Male | 2,840 | | | | | | | |
| Sri Lanka | 12,711 | 1.7 | 200 | 1.1 | 82 | 70 | 47 | 81 |
| Female | 6,185 | | | | 78 | 69 | 43 | 72 |
| Male | 6,525 | | | | 82 | 67 | 52 | 89 |

| | | | | | | | | |
|---|---|---|---|---|---|---|---|---|
| Mexico | 48,225 | 3.4 | 1,090 | 2.3 | 75 | 68 | 66 | 74 |
| Female | 24,159 | | | | 73 | 67 | 65 | 70 |
| Male | 24,065 | | | | 70 | 63 | 77 | 78 |
| United States | 203,235 | 0.6 | 7,890 | 1.6 | 95 | 73 | 15 | 99 |
| Female | 104,299 | | | | 97 | 76 | 16 | 99 |
| Male | 98,912 | | | | 90 | 68 | 21 | 99 |

[a]Population data are for the latest year for which male/female breakdowns are available: Egypt (1976), Kenya (1969), Sudan (1973: no breakdown by sex available), Tunisia (1975), Sri Lanka (1971), Mexico (1970), United States (1970).

[b]The natural increase in the population is defined as the birth rate minus the death rate.

[c]Total figures are mid-1970s. Male/female data are latest available: Egypt (1960), Kenya (1960s), Sudan (no breakdown by sex available), Tunisia (no breakdown by sex available), Sri Lanka (1969), Mexico (1970), United States (1971).

[d]The Physical Quality of Life Index (PQLI) is a composite index based on an average of life expectancy, infant mortality, and literacy. The worst possible performance is one; the best possible performance is 100.

[e]Life expectancy at age one.

SOURCES: Population data are from United Nations, Demographic Yearbook, 1976, Vol. 28 (New York: United Nations, 1977), Table 3, pp. 118-29. Rates of natural increase in population are from Population Reference Bureau, Inc., "1978 World Population Data Sheet" (Washington, D.C.); per capita GNP and per capita GNP growth rate figures as well as total PQLI, life expectancy, infant mortality, and literacy for each country are derived from Martin M. McLaughlin and the Staff of the Overseas Development Council, The United States and World Development: Agenda 1979 (New York: Praeger Publishers, 1979); male and female PQLI, life expectancy, infant mortality, and literacy are from Morris D. Morris, Measuring the Condition of the World's Poor: The Physical Quality of Life Index (New York: Pergamon Press, forthcoming).

*Table 2*
**Illiteracy and Education, by Sex**

| | Percentage of Population Illiterate[a][b] | Percentage of Eligible Age Group in Primary School[c] | Percentage of Eligible Age Group in Secondary School[c] |
|---|---|---|---|
| **Egypt** | | | |
| Female | 88 | 53 | 29 |
| Male | 60 | 79 | 54 |
| **Kenya** | | | |
| Female | 90 | 65 | 7 |
| Male | 70 | 83 | 15 |
| **Sudan** | | | |
| Female | 96 | 26 | 4 |
| Male | 75 | 54 | 12 |
| **Tunisia** | | | |
| Female | 89 | 78 | 13 |
| Male | 63 | 100 | 32 |
| **Sri Lanka** | | | |
| Female | 32 | 98 | 42 |
| Male | 14 | 99 | 45 |
| **Mexico** | | | |
| Female | 30 | { 55 | { 10 |
| Male | 22 | | |
| **United States** | | | |
| Female | 1 | { 95 | { 93 |
| Male | 1 | | |

[a]The illiteracy rate is defined as that proportion of the adult population 15 years or older unable to read or write.
[b]Data are the most recent available; they range between 1960 and 1969.
[c]Data are the most recent available; they range between 1970 and 1975.

SOURCES: Illiteracy data are from U.N. Educational, Scientific, and Cultural Organization, Statistical Yearbook, 1976, Table 1.3, pp. 43-59; data on percentage of population in school from Report on Population and Family Planning (Washington, D.C.: Population Council, October 1976), Table 3, pp. 7-17.

# About the Author
# and Other Contributors

*Perdita Huston* is at present Peace Corps Regional Director for North Africa, the Near East, Asia, and the Pacific. Her interest in world development issues originates in her medical-social work experience in North Africa in the early 1960s. She is the author of *Message from the Village* — a contribution to the population policy debate — published in 1978 by The Epoch B Foundation in cooperation with the U.N. Fund for Population Activities; she has also written for the *New York Times, Life, Populi,* and a number of other publications concerned with development problems and policies.

*Arvonne S. Fraser* is Coordinator of the *Office of Women in Development, U.S. Agency for International Development,* in Washington, D.C. Established as a result of the Percy Amendment to the Foreign Assistance Act of 1973, the Office encourages, assists, and disseminates information about efforts to integrate women and women's concerns into all A.I.D. programs — thus assisting the total development effort and helping to improve women's status.

*Mayra Buvinić* is Acting President of the *International Center for Research on Women.* The ICRW is a nonprofit corporation founded in 1976 to help in the design and implementation of policy and programs that will improve the condition of women, especially impoverished women, in developing countries, and thereby contribute more effectively to overall national and international development efforts. In 1978, ICRW projects have focused on poverty as a women's issue and on the rise of households headed by women in the Third World. The ICRW has a unique library of materials on women and development and publishes a quarterly newsletter.

The *Overseas Development Council* — copublisher and disseminator of this volume — is an independent, nonprofit organization established in 1969 to increase American understanding of the economic and social problems confronting the developing countries, and of the importance of these countries to the United States in an increasingly interdependent world. The ODC seeks to promote consideration of development issues by the American public, policymakers, specialists, educators, and the media through its research, conferences, publications, and liaison with U.S. mass membership organizations interested in U.S. relations with the developing world. The ODC's program is funded by foundations, corporations, and private individuals; its policies are determined by its Board of Directors. Theodore M. Hesburgh, C.S.C., is Chairman of the Board, and Edward J. Schlegel is its Vice Chairman. The Council's President is James P. Grant.

# RELATED TITLES
Published by
Praeger Special Studies

**Titles published in cooperation with the
Overseas Development Council:**

---

**†WOMEN AND WORLD DEVELOPMENT:
WITH AN ANNOTATED BIBLIOGRAPHY**
> edited by Irene Tinker, Michèle Bo Bramsen, and
> Mayra Buvinić

**\*THE UNITED STATES AND WORLD DEVELOPMENT:
AGENDA 1979**
> Martin M. McLaughlin and the Staff
> of the Overseas Development Council

**\*EMPLOYMENT, GROWTH AND BASIC NEEDS:
A ONE-WORLD PROBLEM**
> prepared by the ILO International Labor Office
> with an Introduction by James P. Grant,
> Overseas Development Council

**Other related titles:**

---

**WOMEN'S STATUS AND FERTILITY
IN THE MUSLIM WORLD**
> edited by James Allman

**SEX AND CLASS IN LATIN AMERICA**
> edited by June Nash and
> Helen Icken Safa

**THE FERTILITY OF WORKING WOMEN:
A SYNTHESIS OF INTERNATIONAL RESEARCH**
> edited by Stanley Kupinsky

*\*Also available in paperback as a PSS Student Edition.*
*†Also available in paperback from the Overseas Development Council.*

**PRAEGER PUBLISHERS**
383 Madison Avenue
New York, N.Y. 10017